PREVIOUS: Reindeer cross the
Siberian snow near Oymyakon,
in the U.S.S.R. A young girl atop
one of the animals herds them
forward towards her family's tent
and a break for food and rest.

Red-hot lava from Pu'u 'O' in
Hawai'i Volcanoes National
Park streams over a moonlike
landscape carved from almost 30
years of continuous lava flow.

A YEAR WITH

NATIONAL GEOGRAPHIC

YEARBOOK 2014

NATIONAL GEOGRAPHIC

WASHINGTON, D.C.

A young woman takes part in the traditional three-day water festival in Cox's Bazar, Bangladesh, held annually during the Rakhine New Year as a symbol of washing away the old year.

CONTENTS

A great grey owl, sometimes called the Lapland owl and known for its large facial disc, hunts on the taiga on a misty morning.

A Year With National Geographic

Welcome to an exciting new year with the *National Geographic Yearbook* for 2014 – packed with fascinating facts, discoveries and stunning images from the realms of nature, science, technology, history, travel, space and beyond. As we celebrate another year of adventure and insight, we are thrilled to share highlights and favourite stories from around the world in true National Geographic style.

We've packed this yearbook with breathtaking images by an international team of photographers, as well as spectacular 'Your Shot' images submitted by readers and fans (check out the tiger picture-of-the-year on page 140) and find out how you can enter your own photo (on page 155). Test your knowledge and entertain yourself with fully researched and remarkable stories. For example, did you know that superhuman hearing could be on the horizon? Or that fish with hands 'walk' the Australian deep sea? Do you know the secret to Egyptian architecture? Or coffee's mystical origins?

Each month, you'll find ways to make the National Geographic experience your own. Easy-to-use survival tips prep you for the great outdoors – nearby or far away. A spotlight on amazing animals inspires awe for every species (see page 145 for a goat who takes rock climbing to new extremes). Whether you're learning local birdcalls or sharing trivia with friends (who knew that one day on the planet Mercury lasts 59 Earth days?), there's something special for everyone.

As you enjoy this year's *Yearbook,* please know that National Geographic is committed to bringing you the best of the world all year round. Happy adventures and best wishes for 2014!

–Janet Goldstein

Senior Vice President and Editorial Director, National Geographic Books

Barren trees protrude from an ethereally blue pond under a thin dusting of snow near Biei on Hokkaidō, Japan's north island.

JANUARY BRINGS THE SNOW, / MAKES OUR FEET AND FINGERS GLOW

JANUARY

Kingston, Jamaica

The third largest island in the Caribbean, after Cuba and Hispaniola, Jamaica offers an array of waterfalls and mountains, fascinating historic sites and beautiful beaches.

Mist settles over Portland parish against the backdrop of Jamaica's Blue Mountains, where the lush vegetation is home to a thriving ecosystem.

Kingston, the nation's vibrant capital, throbs with the energy of more than half a million citizens. The heart of the city lies downtown near the waterfront, with historic sites such as the former British army parade grounds and the submerged city of Port Royal.

With temperatures averaging 25–30°C (77–86°F) year-round, a visit to the nearby beaches is practically a mandate. A few miles to the north, Turtle Beach teems with activity. Dive in to your choice of water sports, relax under an umbrella or check out the local shopping scene. Neighbouring Ocho Rios – a favourite cruise ship destination – is known for its overwhelming natural wonders, including a 180-metre-long (600-foot) cascade.

Across the eastern part of the country lies igneous rock deposited by a broad arc of volcanoes that rose from the seabed billions of years ago. Today, the Blue Mountains and their misty peaks are home to a diverse ecosystem, as well as the source of some of the world's most prized coffee. ▥

Is That a Banana in Your Water?

Banana peels are no longer just for composting or comedy shows: new science shows they can pull heavy-metal contamination from river water. The fruit's peel even outperforms traditional water remediation strategies, providing a higher extraction capacity without any negative side effects to the water source.

An Emotional Aphrodisiac

Mouse
Mus musculus
SIZE: 12.7 – 23 cm
WEIGHT: 17 – 22 g
RANGE: Subspecies can be found across the world

A guy who can shed a tear can drive females wild – among mice, at least.

According to a new study, male mouse tears contain a sex pheromone called ESP1, which makes female mice more receptive to mounting. While sex pheromones are known to have similar effects in other animals, the study shows how the interaction works 'at the molecular level and also the brain level,' says study co-author Kazushige Touhara of the University of Tokyo.

Male mice shed tears to keep their eyes from drying out. As they groom themselves, the tears – and the pheromone – get spread around their bodies and nests. When female mice come in contact with a male or his nest, they pick up the pheromone via a nose organ called the vomeronasal, where the pheromone binds to a specific protein receptor.

'She has to touch it,' Touhara explains, 'because this is not a volatile compound like a fragrance,' referring to the ease with which some other chemicals turn into vapour. Upon contact, the pheromone is sent to sex-specific regions in the female's brain. The female mouse is then three times more likely to engage in what's called lordosis behaviour, a posture shown by many animals in heat in which they thrust their rumps and tails upward.

Humans lack the gene that codes for ESP1 and its receptor, Touhara notes, so men are unlikely to gain a sexual edge – chemically speaking – if they decide to show their more sensitive side. ∎

Thanks to the sex pheromones in their tears, male mice are more likely to drive females to engage in mating behaviours when they shed a few.

STRANGE ... BUT TRUE! A mouse's heart is shorter than a Tic Tac and beats an average of 480 to 600 times per minute at rest.

At a metre (3 feet) tall, emperor penguins are the largest species of penguin. The remarkable swimmers are capable of diving more than 500 metres (1,640 feet).

Instinctual Cravings

In your brain the harmless craving for crisps or other salty snacks, scientists have found, may share pathways with dangerous addictions to drugs.

Drugs such as heroin and cocaine may owe some of their addictive powers to an ancient instinct: our appetite for salt. In a new study of mouse brains, scientists have shown that the patterns of gene regulation stimulated by salt cravings are the same gene patterns regulated by drug addiction. Salt appetite is a craving millions of years in the making, with likely roots in the salty seas where life on Earth began. 'Land dwellers face a problem in that sodium is a trace element, so they have to have a strategy to ingest sodium, and salt craving or sodium appetite is evolution's answer to that,' explains study co-author Wolfgang Liedtke, an assistant professor of medicine and neurobiology at Duke University.

Salt appetite can be so strong that animals short on sodium will put life and limb at risk to satisfy the hunger. Mountain goats, for instance, are known to cling to sheer cliffs to access a salt lick, even when a misstep means certain death.

The new finding suggests that drug addictions may be so hard to overcome in part because cocaine and opiates – both derived from plants – exploit the brain mechanisms critical for salt appetite. 'Cocaine can usurp the ancient [neural] systems that have made animals better survivors,' Liedtke says.

Overall, though, Liedtke cautions that the new study doesn't fully explain the neural drivers of drug addiction. 'Sodium appetite is a healthy instinct; heroin addiction is a disease that can kill a human,' he notes. 'To go from a healthy instinct to a malady – other things must be happening in the brain.' ▤

Recovery It's possible that this research may lead to new treatments for drug addiction that don't rely on 'cold turkey' abstinence, which is less likely to be successful against strong, instinctual cravings.

Wang Cai:
Patience Is a Virtue

Queuing at the bank is up there with life's more tedious tasks. But imagine waiting *outside* the bank . . . for eight hours. That's what Wang Cai, a Pomeranian mix in Chongqing, China, has done every day for four years, spending his days watching the world go by while his owner is working inside. Dressed in a snazzy red-and-black coat, the petite Wang Cai greets passersby with charm. Other dogs get chased away, but Wang Cai rarely leaves his post on the steps of the Minsheng bank.

Canine expert and trainer Philip Levine is hardly surprised by Wang Cai's behaviour, despite the fact that his owner says she neither asked nor trained the dog to wait for her. 'Dogs are creatures of survival and identify a person who is benevolent, who provides food, shelter and identification,' Levine explains. And Wang Cai, who was originally found wandering the streets, knows he has a good thing going. ▮

A most patient Pomeranian: Wang Cai loyally sits outside the Minsheng bank, waiting for his owner to complete another day's work.

How To: Make Your Own Snowshoes

For wintry emergencies, these shoes simplify walking and pulling loads in deep snow.

1 Find two densely needled pine branches of equal size, about 80 to 90 centimetres (2.5 to 3.0 feet) in length.

2 For each branch, tie a long cord or strong grasses around the thickest part of the branch, about three to five centimetres (an inch or two) from the end. Leave enough rope loose to attach your boot to the branch.

3 Loop the cord on both sides underneath the first boughs. Put your foot on the body of the branch, with your toe closest to the end where the knot is tied. Tie your boot into place by looping the rope around your toe and heel and knotting securely.

EXPERT TIP: To walk, stride by lifting the toe up above the snow, then pushing your foot forward. Firmly plant the leading snowshoe, shift your weight onto it and pause an instant after each step.

Anatomy of the Mosh Pit: When Things Get Rowdy

Parents may never understand their rock 'n' roll-loving children, but scientists might.

To most scientists, 'heavy metal' refers to elements on the lower end of the periodic table. But to Jesse Silverberg and Matt Bierbaum, doctoral students at Cornell University's department of Condensed Matter Physics, the aggressive music known as heavy metal – and the violent dancing that accompanies it – could be a key to understanding extreme situations such as riots and panicked responses to disasters.

For the past two years, Silverberg and Bierbaum have studied 'moshing' at heavy metal concerts, using theories of collective motion and the physical properties of gasses to better understand the chaos of metal fans' dancing. Moshing, for those who have never attended a heavy metal concert, is a form of dancing in which participants bump, jostle and slam into one another.

Silverberg and Bierbaum think it can also be understood by applying models of gaseous particles. As these particles

Moshing is comparable to the 'flocking' behaviour of animals.

float in groups, they too run, bash and slam into each other, sending the elements flying in chaotic patterns. 'We are interested in how humans behave in similar excited states,' says Silverberg.

Mosh pits provided the scientists with a way to observe excited collective movement without causing undue injury or death. Analysing hours of recorded footage from concerts and making multiple field trips to music clubs, the scientists

recognised the particulate physical patterns in the mosh pit.

Furthermore, they differentiated two distinct forms of heavy metal dancing: the mosh pit itself, which follows the gaseous pattern, and the 'circle pit' – where dancers run, smash and dance in a circular rotation – within it, which adheres to a vortex pattern of particulate behaviour.

'Herd animals behave in very similar spirit – what physicists call "flocking" behaviour,' notes Bierbaum. As with groups of flying birds or schooling fish, simple rules can be applied to individuals in large groups – like moshers – to understand what seems to be very complex behaviour. This makes modelling possible, allowing computers to re-create immense numbers of actions in a matter of seconds. These models can then be used to design spaces that would minimise trampling or injury or to tailor responses to disasters like fires. ▪

Spirit Dance Anthropologists who studied moshing as a social ritual have likened it to a form of spirit possession in its uncontrolled, dynamic and often violent nature.

Scientists investigating the phenomenon of moshing have made multiple field trips to heavy metal concerts and clubs to identify the patterns of movement involved.

The Hengifoss waterfall in Iceland pours over the Litlanesfoss waterfall, flanked by remarkable hexagonal columns formed from solidified basalt lava.

Fireworks

Fireworks were discovered at least 1,000 years ago when a Chinese cook accidentally mixed saltpetre, sulphur and charcoal. When compressed into a bamboo tube, the mixture exploded. No one has explained why a cook might have tamped this volatile compound into a tube, though.

The Chinese themselves credit fireworks to a monk named Li Tian and honour him every year on 18 April. The Chinese used fireworks and firecrackers, calling them *yanhua* or 'smoke flowers,' to frighten off evil spirits. Marco Polo and Christian crusaders brought gunpowder back to Europe, where many nations discovered a passion for fireworks. These 'flying arrows of fire' soon became an integral part of New Year's Eve, weddings and other celebrations. ▦

Greater White-Fronted Goose

Anser albifrons

LENGTH: 65–78 cm
WINGSPAN: 135–165 cm

A bird of the open steppe and farmland in winter months, the greater white-fronted goose has a noisy voice with a typical goose-type cackling. Characteristic flight sounds include repeated musical *lyolyok*s of a higher pitch than those of bean or greylag geese, but less shrill than the pink-footed. ▦

Strange ... But True: The Human Body

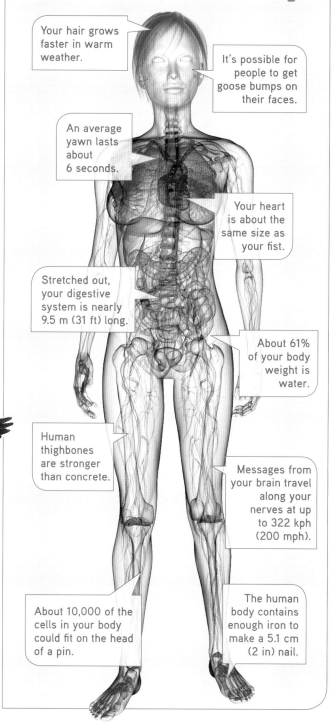

Your hair grows faster in warm weather.

It's possible for people to get goose bumps on their faces.

An average yawn lasts about 6 seconds.

Your heart is about the same size as your fist.

Stretched out, your digestive system is nearly 9.5 m (31 ft) long.

About 61% of your body weight is water.

Human thighbones are stronger than concrete.

Messages from your brain travel along your nerves at up to 322 kph (200 mph).

About 10,000 of the cells in your body could fit on the head of a pin.

The human body contains enough iron to make a 5.1 cm (2 in) nail.

A daredevil skier launches
himself from a snowy
cliff high up in dangerous
mountain terrain.

WAN FEBRUARY WITH WEEPING CHEER, / WHOSE COLD HAND GUIDES THE YOUNGLING YEAR

BRUARY

Preda to Bergün, Switzerland

Switzerland's largest and most scenic canton, Graubünden is favoured for its varied outdoor activities and bracing clean air.

Joy ride: experience the thrills and spills of Europe's longest floodlit sledge run, which stretches across Switzerland's Graubünden region.

Stretching across 6 kilometres (3.7 miles) of the sparsely populated Graubünden region, the Preda–Bergün cross-country toboggan course is Switzerland's first and Europe's longest floodlit sledge run. Take the Rhaetian Railway to the tiny village of Preda (about 20 minutes from St. Moritz and 3 hours from Zurich), rent a wooden sledge at the train station and hold on tight for the exhilarating plunge down the closed Abula Pass road from Preda (1,800 metres/5,900 feet above sea level) to the finish at Bergün (1,367 metres/4,484 feet).

The icy course winds through towering pine trees and past tidy Swiss farms and villages. Periodic total darkness adds to the adventure and danger. Wear a ski helmet and goggles for safety, and watch for riders pitched off their sleds on hairpin turns. Snowmaking equipment helps ensure a full season of sledding, but check weather conditions and operating hours before making the train trek to Preda – a breathtaking adventure in itself. ▮

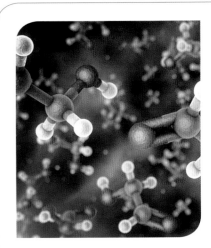

An Intergalactic Treat

Astronomers have made a sweet discovery: simple sugar molecules floating in the gas around a star some 400 light-years away, suggesting the possibility of life on other planets. Known as glycoaldehyde, the carbon-rich molecules are believed to play a key role in the chemical reaction that forms ribonucleic acid (RNA), a crucial biomolecule present in all living cells.

Small but Mighty: Ants Use Teamwork to Survive

Fire Ant
Solenopsis invicta
SIZE: 0.24 – 0.6 cm
WEIGHT: 3 mg +
RANGE: Native to South America, U.S., Australia

When a city floods, humans stack sandbags and raise levees. When a fire ant colony floods, the ants link up to form a literal life raft.

When floodwaters strike, fire ants of the species *Solenopsis invicta* react with a clever escape plan: within minutes, colony members link together to form a water-repellent raft that can stay afloat for weeks.

Intrigued, Georgia Tech researchers studied in the lab how the insects, native to South America and now roaming the southern United States, interlock claws, mandibles and sticky pads on their legs to construct the roughly circular rafts. Air bubbles trapped among the ants' bodies and hairs create buoyancy for the two-tiered structure and enable members on its underside to breathe.

Colonies of as many as 200,000 ants can form rafts measuring up to half a metre (2 feet) wide. And in a remarkable feat of swarm intelligence that helps maintain the raft's integrity, ants on the bottom quickly move on top when others succumb to encounters with debris, predators or swift currents, observes researcher Nathan Mlot. Scientists believe that studying this superorganism could provide valuable new insights into microrobotics and improved water repellency.

1: By grasping one another with jaws, legs and sticky pads, fire ants form a raft to ride out floods. The raft's rough and irregular shape increases water resistance.

2: On the raft's underside, air bubbles trapped among the bodies create a pocket that enables the ants to breathe and keeps the structure afloat. ▦

Five hundred South American fire ants assemble into a buoyant raft during a lab investigation into their behaviour.

STRANGE ... BUT TRUE! A species of carpenter ants in Southeast Asia makes itself explode when attacked.

Is Your Brain Sleeping While You're Awake?

If you think you can function on minimal sleep, here's a wake-up call: parts of your brain may doze off even if you're totally awake.

Sleep deprivation can do strange things to a brain – including putting it on auto-pilot without your knowledge. In a recent study, scientists observed the electrical activity of brains in rats forced to stay awake longer than usual. Problem-solving brain regions fell into a kind of 'local sleep' – which the study authors believe is a condition likely in sleep-deprived humans, too.

Surprisingly, when sections of the rats' brains entered these sleeplike states, 'you couldn't tell that [the rats were] in any way in a different state of wakefulness,' says study co-author Giulio Tononi, a neuroscientist at the University of Wisconsin, Madison. This phenomenon of local sleep 'actually affects behaviour,' according to Tononi. For example, when the scientists had the rats perform a challenging task – using their paws to reach sugar pellets – the sleep-deprived animals had trouble completing it.

The researchers used toys to distract the rats into staying awake for a few hours. The team discovered that neurons – the nerve cells that collect and transmit signals in the brain – in two sections of these overtired rats' cerebral cortices entered a slow-wave stage that is essentially sleep.

It's still unknown why parts of an awake brain nod off. One leading theory holds that, since neurons are constantly 'recording' new information, at some point the neurons need to 'turn off' in order to reset themselves and prepare to learn again. 'If this hypothesis is correct,' Tononi says, 'that means that at some point [if you're putting off sleep], you're beginning to overwhelm your neurons.' So the neurons 'take the rest, even if they shouldn't' – and there's a price to pay in terms of making 'stupid' errors, Tononi warns. ▮

Truth: Staying awake for 24 hours impairs hand-to-eye coordination as much as having a blood alcohol content of 0.1 per cent.

Schwani:
A Regular Casanova

At home in Velen, Germany, Schwani the swan is inseparable from the love of his life – a blue 39 horsepower tractor.

Schwani the swan is head over webbed feet in love. He spends his days at his home in Velen, Germany, following his sweetheart around. Unfortunately, his crush doesn't pay him much attention.

The swan has been devoted to Hermann-Josef Hericks's tractor ever since Hericks, groundskeeper at the hotel where Schwani lives, bought it three years ago. Whenever he takes the vehicle for a spin, Schwani waddles close behind. If Hericks stops the machine, the swan stands beside it, sometimes trying to jump on the seat. 'We even park the tractor outside so Schwani can sit next to it,' Hericks says.

Why would a swan be so attached to a tractor? 'Newborn birds follow the first thing they see,' wildlife expert Julia Newth explains. 'It's called imprinting. Schwani probably saw or heard a tractor in the first few days of his life.' Maybe it's not true love, but the tractor is still very important to Schwani. Says Hericks, 'I just can't imagine him without it.'

How To: Ice-Fish

Even in subzero conditions, it's possible to land a big one (no, *this* big) with the right strategy.

1 Use an auger or ice chisel to cut holes in ice over water.

2 Rig line and bait to the end of one of a pair of sticks that are crossed in a plus-sign shape and tied tightly at their intersection. Set the sticks over the hole to rotate when the bait is pulled down.

3 Keep holes from freezing shut by covering them at night with brush and snow.

4 The baited stick pops up when a fish bites.

EXPERT TIP: There are several sources of food in the Arctic and subarctic regions. The type of food – fish, animal, fowl or plant – and the ease in obtaining it depend on the time of the year and your location.

A magical night in Jackson, Wyoming. Locals believe that ice crystals in the frigid air refracted the town's lights to create the dazzling effect.

High-Tech Heroes

In the Atlantic Ocean, locating a right whale *(Eubalaena glacialis)* the size of a school bus can be like finding a needle in a haystack. But a new generation of sharp-eared underwater robots can pinpoint the leviathans' locations in real time.

In 2012, two 1.8-metre-long (6-foot), torpedo-shaped robots from the Woods Hole Oceanographic Institution (WHOI) in Massachusetts used digital acoustic monitoring equipment to detect nine North Atlantic right whales in the Gulf of Maine – the first-ever detection of baleen whales from these types of autonomous vehicles.

'Recording the sound creates a spectrogram, which to a scientist is almost like a sheet of music that visually represents the sounds you're hearing,' explained WHOI researcher Mark Baumgartner.

The gliders process and classify these acoustic signatures, then surface every two hours and transmit evidence of whale calls to shore-based computers while the animals are still nearby. 'We can use this information to very quickly draw a circle on the map and say, hey, we know there are whales in this area,

One of the underwater robots used to detect whales

let's be careful about our activities here,' says Baumgartner. 'The government can then alert mariners and ask them to reduce their speed and post a lookout.'

On 5 December 2012, one such glider enabled the National Oceanic and Atmospheric Administration's Fisheries Service to alert mariners to 70-ton whales in the Outer Fall area, some 100 kilometres (60 miles) south of Bar Harbor, Maine and 145 kilometres (90 miles) northeast of Portsmouth, New Hampshire.

Ship collisions are a major source of mortality for the critically endangered right whales, accounting for perhaps a third of all known deaths. Devastated by whaling, the species has been slow to recover – less than 500 right whales remain and biologists stress that each living animal's survival is important for the future of the species.

The robots' acoustic system is also very flexible. While currently armed with data to detect right, humpback, fin and sei whales, new sounds and species could be added that would enable the gliders to travel widely in search of other marine creatures.

The gliders can work at sea for four or five weeks before their batteries need recharging. If money and management priorities allowed, one could imagine a fleet of such vessels one day cruising constantly and collecting valuable data on whales and other marine animals.

The underwater robots also boast a suite of environmental sensors to record temperature and salinity and to estimate algae population levels at the base of the marine food chain – valuable tools that could provide insight as to *why* the animals are in a particular area.

A rare southern right whale. These leviathans are known for their enormous heads, which can measure up to one-third of their total body length.

Red peppers are laid out to dry in the sun in India's Rajasthan province, before being ground into a spicy powder used in curries.

Red Roses

The tribute of red roses for a loved one has a long and colourful history. One legend maintains that red roses came about when Eve kissed a white rose in the Garden of Eden. Another legend has it that Harpocrates, god of silence, happened upon Venus, goddess of love, in the act of lovemaking. Cupid, Venus's son, bribed him into silence by giving him the first rose in the world.

Dionysius the Younger, tyrant of Syracuse (fourth century B.C.), ordered his house filled with roses for the parties he had with young women of the city. The wealthy Romans would lie on beds of roses, wearing garlands and crowns of roses. The ancient Romans so loved roses that they imported them in barges from Egypt, and when the growing season was over they filled their fountains with rosewater.

Scops Owl

Otus scops
LENGTH: 19–20 cm
WINGSPAN: 53–63 cm

The smallest owl of the region, this nocturnal bird inhabits open, broadleaved woodland, groves, orchards, parks and large gardens. The mating call of the male is a short, clear whistle, *tyuu*, monotonously repeated every three seconds – not to be confused with the similar but shorter sounds made by midwife toads. The call is often heard in a long, drawn-out duet with the softer, higher-pitched call of the female, which tends to be larger than the males of their species.

Strange ... But True:
Sweets

A 5,000-year-old piece of chewing gum was discovered in Finland.

+220,052
A British chocolate company created a giant box of chocolates filled with 220,052 individual chocolates.

+ ♥♥♥
Chewing gum can make your heart beat faster.

A British confectioner once created a 2.9-metre-tall (9.5 foot) billboard made entirely of chocolate.

£££££
A 100-year-old chocolate bar sold for nearly £463.

The oldest chocolate ever found was inside a 2,600-year-old pot in Belize.

🚚🚚🚚🚚🚚🚚🚚 =
A baking company created a chocolate chip cookie that weighed as much as 7 pickup trucks.

The largest pumpkin pie weighed 916 kg (2,020 lb).

The first candy canes were made without stripes.

A piece of cake more than 4,000 years old was found in a tomb in Egypt.

Blooming tulips herald the coming of springtime in Hershey Gardens, Pennsylvania.

FAR-OFF, UNSEEN, SPRING FAINTLY CRIES, / BIDDING HER EARLIEST CHILD ARISE

MARCH

Parque Nacional Volcán Arenal, Costa Rica

Studded by a string of volcanoes, Costa Rica's cowboy country abounds in dramatic landscapes, from dry deciduous woodlands to mist-shrouded cloud forests.

The thousand-year-old Arenal volcano in Costa Rica lights up the night sky with an impressive pyrotechnic show.

Volcán Arenal (1,643 metres/5,389 feet) is a quintessential cone volcano and the focus of its namesake national park, Parque Nacional Volcán Arenal of the north-western Guanacaste region. Arenal began to emerge about 1,000 years ago, pushing up like a great molehill. On 29 July 1968, a fateful earthquake awakened the slumbering giant and it has simmered ever since. Barely a day goes by without a minor eruption; there are usually blocks of smoke rolling down the slopes. It is especially spectacular at night, when the pyrotechnics appear like a giant firecracker and red-hot lava oozes down the steep slopes.

Explore the flanks' spectacular scenery on horseback during the day, or slip into one of the soothing hot springs nearby. The 12,080-hectare (29,850-acre) park is made up of 16 protected reserves and is also home to Volcán Chato – Arenal's dormant sibling with a pea-green lagoon pooling in its collapsed crater. Dry season (November to April) is the best time to visit. ▓

BOTANY

I Think I'm a Clone Now

The peat moss *Sphagnum palustre* is found throughout the northern hemisphere, but the Hawaiian variety appears to reproduce only through cloning. The moss populations sampled in a new study suggest that the little green organisms descended from a single founder plant that was carried via wind to Hawaii.

Look, Ma! They've Got Hands!

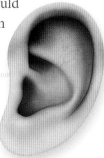

Pink Handfish
Brachiopsilus dianthus
SIZE: 10 – 14 cm
RANGE: Eastern
Indian Ocean,
Australia, Tasmania

Not much for swimming, the handfish family uses their fins to walk along the ocean floor.

All of the world's 14 known species of handfish are found only in shallow coastal waters off southeastern Australia. But about 50 million years ago, the animals likely inhabited regions around the world, as noted by Australia's Commonwealth Scientific and Industrial Research Organisation scientists. Fossils of the curious creatures have been discovered in the Mediterranean, for example

Scientists have announced nine newly named species in a recent scientific review of the handfish family based on fin rays, colouration and other criteria. Here are two of our favourites:

Fish #1: New, Pink and Rare
Only four specimens of the elusive 10-centimetre (4-inch) pink handfish have ever been found, and all of those were collected from areas around the city of Hobart on the Australian island of Tasmania. Though no one has spotted a living pink handfish since 1999, it's taken until now for scientists to formally identify it as a unique species.

Fish #2: See Spot Walk
The spotted handfish is found on sandy sediments at the bottom of Tasmania's Derwent Estuary and adjoining bays. The fish use their fins to walk along the seabed, where they eat small invertebrates such as worms. Researchers think that the slow-moving species has a secret weapon against prowling predators: a toxic skin that could lead to death within an hour of ingestion. ▦

Today the elusive handfish is found only in Australia's coastal waters, but the species may have inhabited seafloors as far away as that of the Mediterranean in prehistoric times.

STRANGE ... BUT TRUE! A 370-million-year-old fish fossil proves that human ears evolved from ancient fish gills.

Mark of Youth

A sassy little mole like Marilyn Monroe's has long been associated with beauty. Now research at King's College London suggests another connection. People with more than a hundred moles may age more slowly than others, perhaps resulting in fewer wrinkles and a reduced risk of osteoporosis.

The reason involves segments of DNA called telomeres, which may shrink over time. Having many moles indicates longer telomeres. This helps put off the moment when some cells are no longer able to divide and renew tissues. It may also make 'moley' people – as many as 10 per cent of Caucasians – prone to cancers, warns lead scientist Veronique Bataille, a dermatologist, but the benefits can sometimes outweigh the risk. 'I tell patients to be vigilant, but consider the positive side of having moles.'

The effects of the aging process are manifold: skin loses its ability to retain moisture; the dermis loses its elasticity and its collagen stretches; and lines and wrinkles from laughter and other habitual facial expressions deepen. To counter these effects, consumers worldwide spend several billion pounds a year on skin care products, not even including skin care services like facials. Most is spent by women, but marketers now target men, as well as girls as young as eight, encouraging them to try to prevent or diminish signs of aging.

Moles or no moles, the wisdom behind maintaining healthy skin remains much the same: to fight wrinkles, hydrate. Wash well, but not with harsh cleansers. And use absorbable antioxidants, such as vitamins A, C and E, which may counteract free-radical damage caused by the sun and natural aging. ▥

Mole or Freckle?
A mole is a cluster of pigment-producing cells that appears as a defined, sometimes raised dot. A freckle is a splotch of pigment, often a sign of sun damage.

Luna:
Putting the Moo in 'Cool Moooves'

L una the cow really stands out from the herd. The German bovine not only lets her 16-year-old owner ride on her back – Luna can also leap over hurdles.

Regina Mayer decided to try 'cow-back riding' with Luna after she was told she couldn't have a horse. Regina began training the farm animal by taking her for long walks. Then she saddled Luna and carefully rode her around. Once Luna got the hang of riding, she was ready for another challenge – jumping.

After months of practice and plenty of treats, the cow could leap over obstacles. Now Luna loves to show off her horselike moves and even responds to commands such as 'go', 'stand' and 'gallop'.

'Cows are intelligent animals,' says veterinarian Owen Rae of the University of Florida. 'With repetitive coaching and a caring trainer, they can learn to do a lot.' In other words, these gals are *udder*-ly amazing. ▥

The cow who jumped: Regina Mayer rides Luna over a homemade hurdle of beer crates and logs at her family's farm in southern Germany.

How To: Make a Compass

Exploring is all about straying from the beaten path, but it's important to know your bearings.

1 Smoothly stroke a needle or razor blade in one direction 50 to 100 times with a piece of silk or magnet.

2 Tie a piece of thread around the middle of the needle.

3 Dangle the needle and it will swing to point towards magnetic north.

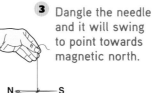

4 Alternative: Float a magnetised needle in a bowl or pool of water by placing the needle on top of a bit of light organic matter.

EXPERT TIP: Humans tend to veer slightly to the left or right as they walk as a result of imbalance – the difference in the length of their legs and favouring their dominant eye – so be sure to check your bearings continually.

Pioneering rock climber and BASE jumper Dean Potter walks across a slackline as the moon rises over Cathedral Peak in Yosemite National Park.

What Makes Us Human? Cooking, Study Says

Did you eat a hot meal today? It's a smart thing to do, as our ancestors learned.

According to a study, a surge in human brain size that occurred roughly 1.8 million years ago can be directly linked to the innovation of cooking. *Homo erectus,* considered the first modern human species, learned to cook and doubled its brain size over the course of 600,000 years. Similar size primates – gorillas, chimpanzees and other great apes, all of which subsisted on a diet of raw foods – did not.

'Much more than harnessing fire, what truly allowed us to become human was using fire for cooking,' suggests study co-author Suzana Herculano-Houzel, a neuroscientist at the Institute of Biomedical Sciences at the Federal University of Rio de Janeiro in Brazil.

Herculano-Houzel and colleague Karina Fonseca-Azevedo measured the body and brain masses of primates and compared them with their caloric intake and hours spent eating. Unsurprisingly, the results showed a direct correlation between calories and body mass. In other words, the bigger you are, the more you have to eat. And given that brain matter 'costs' more calories than other body mass, according to the 'expensive tissue hypothesis', gorillas could never eat enough nutrients to support their enormous size.

Humans couldn't either. But when we came to a fork in the evolutionary road – brawn this way, brains that way – we took the cerebral route. This development came to be known as encephalization: we ended up with brains that are much bigger than our body size would indicate. How is that possible?

Cooking was the key, Herculano-Houzel believes. Heating our food unlocked nutrition: 100 per cent of a cooked meal is metabolised by the body, whereas raw foods yield just 30 or 40 per cent of their nutrients. Applying fire to food also softens tough fibres and speeds up the process of chewing and digesting, so that our ancestors could spend less time searching for nourishment and more time developing other interests.

Is there still room for us to evolve? Herculano-Houzel thinks so. Human brain size 'may not be capped out yet,' she says. 'Over the last couple of centuries, our body size has increased due mainly to changes in our diet, to increased access to better nutrition.' She speculates that we could continue to evolve bigger and bigger brains – with the right diet. What exactly *that* is, however, is still a matter of taste. ▮

Evolving or Devolving? Cooking might increase nutritional yield, but too much highly caloric, immediately gratifying food can be dangerous, too. Diseases such as obesity, hypertension, diabetes and heart disease are all connected to overindulging our taste for refined sugars and processed foods.

Mabenda, the western lowland gorilla, munches on grass. Scientists theorise that learning to cook was key in separating early humans from apes.

Coloured powder flies during
Holi, the festival of colours,
in Dhaka, Bangladesh.
Hindus observe the vibrant
celebration every spring.

St. Patrick's Day

17 March, the day that traditionally celebrates St. Patrick (c. 389–461), the patron saint of Ireland, is known for spirited parades, beer drinking and the wearing of anything green. Although many legends concerning St. Patrick have proliferated since his death, he was a real person who in about 450 left a credible account of his life entitled *Confessio.* Born in Britain, Patrick was kidnapped by pirates at age 16 and sold into slavery in Ireland. After six years, he escaped back to Britain and then to France. There, he dreamed he received a letter, 'The Voice of the Irish', imploring him to return to Ireland as a missionary. After a period of study, he heeded the call, remaining there for the rest of his life and sharing Catholicism with many thousands of people. ▨

Ruddy Turnstone

Arenaria interpres
LENGTH: 21–25 cm
WINGSPAN: 50–57 cm

A sociable bird, the ruddy turnstone gives a staccato rattle of clear, short nasal notes – *tuk, tuk-i-tuk-tuk* – while in flight. Alarm calls include a sharp *teu* and, especially during breeding season, a strong *TIT-wooTITwoooRITitititititit,* ending in a rolling chatter. The stocky, smallish wader favours rocky shores, both along coasts and estuaries. ▨

Strange ... But True: Sports

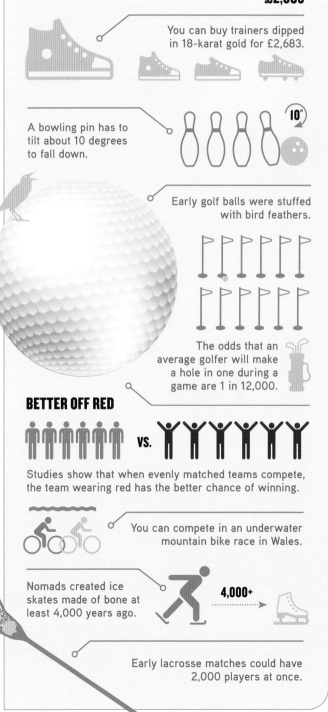

£2,683

You can buy trainers dipped in 18-karat gold for £2,683.

A bowling pin has to tilt about 10 degrees to fall down.

10°

Early golf balls were stuffed with bird feathers.

The odds that an average golfer will make a hole in one during a game are 1 in 12,000.

BETTER OFF RED

VS.

Studies show that when evenly matched teams compete, the team wearing red has the better chance of winning.

You can compete in an underwater mountain bike race in Wales.

Nomads created ice skates made of bone at least 4,000 years ago.

4,000+

Early lacrosse matches could have 2,000 players at once.

A grasshopper feeds on the
pollen of a brilliant daylily,
so named for its bloom that
lasts only 24 hours.

AGAIN THE BLACKBIRDS SING; THE STREAMS / WAKE, LAUGHING, FROM THEIR WINTER DREAMS

APRIL

Danube Delta, Romania

Situated in the country's south-eastern region, the Danube Delta is the third most important wetland in the world. The wealth of animals and plant life will amaze and astound.

This vividly coloured kingfisher is just one of 300 species of bird who inhabit the sprawling sandbanks and reed beds of Romania's Danube Delta.

The Secret Language of Stripes

A skunk's stripes aren't just for style – they may direct predators' eyes right to the source of the animal's smelly anal spray, which helps tell them 'Stay away!' A study of nearly 200 carnivorous mammals shows that fighters tend to be more boldly coloured than more peaceable animals, which tend to use camouflage to stay safe.

Covering nearly 5,800 square kilometres (2,000 square miles) of sandy islands, floating reed beds, dikes, forest and marsh, the Danube Delta is the youngest part of Romania. It formed only 13,000 years ago, when the Gulf of Tulcea silted up. Large vessels can navigate only three of the thousands of waterways and lakes that crisscross the land. The dynamic delta's sandbanks and reed beds constantly shift as the river deposits millions of tons of mud and silt here, at the end of its 2,860-kilometre (1,788-mile) journey to the Black Sea.

More than 300 species of bird – including white pelican, glossy ibis, swans and squacco heron – either live in or visit the delta, which is also home to 45 species of freshwater fish. The most relaxing way to take it all in is by boat; there are several tourist-friendly fishing villages from which to disembark. Caraorman village – with its fetching, reed-roofed houses and a fleet of wooden fishing boats called *lotci* – is a great jumping-off point. ▇

Spawn of Medieval 'Black Death' Bug Still Roam the Earth

The Black Death killed millions of people in medieval Europe and continues to kill today. But another epidemic remains unlikely, because recent studies show that the plague bacterium has changed little in the last 600 years.

The new findings are based on bacteria recovered from skeletons found in a mid-1300s cemetery for Black Death victims in London. The grave excavation was undertaken by the Museum of London Archaeology. After examining samples of *Yersinia pestis* – the genome of the Black Death pathogen – from 46 teeth and 53 bones recovered from the site, the research team determined that the plague hasn't changed much, genetically speaking, in more than six centuries.

Once infected with *Y. pestis,* a person can develop bubonic plague, an infection of the lymph nodes, or the rarer pneumonic plague, a secondary infection of the lungs. When the plague arrived in Europe in the 1340s, it killed as many as 30 to 50 million people – up to half the continent's population – in five years.

Today, the plague is still spread mainly by fleas on burrowing rodents.

The 'Black Death' first struck medieval England in 1348, devastating the population.

The disease hits up to 3,000 people worldwide each year – most commonly in the United States, Asia and South America. With treatment, 85 per cent of modern victims survive. The fact that the bacterial genome has been slow to change suggests that modern medical knowledge and general susceptibility – not a less virulent version of *Y. pestis* – may be why the plague no longer devastates populations. ▐

STRANGE ... BUT TRUE! Due to the plague's slow evolution, today's antibiotics are effective against modern *Y. pestis* and they would have been effective against the Black Death, too.

Vampire Forensics: Skull of the Undead

A skull unearthed in Italy reveals the very real belief in medieval vampires.

Among the many medieval plague victims recently unearthed near Venice, Italy, one reportedly had never-before-seen evidence of an unusual affliction: being 'undead'. The partial body and skull of the woman showed her jaw forced open by a brick – an exorcism technique used on suspected vampires.

It's the first time that archaeological remains have been interpreted as belonging to a suspected vampire, team leader Matteo Borrini, a forensic archaeologist at the University of Florence, told National Geographic News. Since 2006, Borrini has been digging up mass graves on the island of Lazzaretto Nuovo, where the supposed vampire was found.

Belief in vampires was rampant in the Middle Ages, mostly because the process of decomposition was not well understood. For instance, as the human stomach decays, it releases a dark 'purge fluid'. This bloodlike liquid can flow freely from a corpse's nose and mouth and it was sometimes imagined to be traces of vampire victims' blood.

The fluid could also moisten the burial shroud near the corpse's mouth enough that it sagged into the jaw, creating tears in the cloth. Since tombs were often reopened during plagues so other victims could be added, Borrini says, Italian gravediggers saw these decomposing bodies with what appeared to be partially eaten shrouds.

Vampires were thought by some to be causes of plagues, Borrini explains, and the superstition took root that shroud chewing was the 'magical way' that vampires spread pestilence. Inserting objects such as bricks or stones into the mouths of alleged vampires was thought to halt the disease. ▥

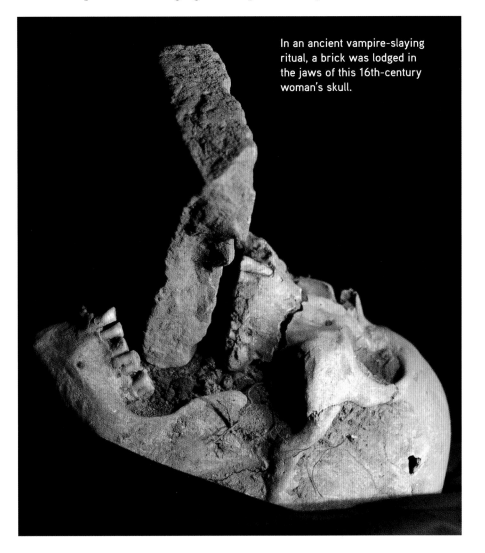

In an ancient vampire-slaying ritual, a brick was lodged in the jaws of this 16th-century woman's skull.

Picasso:
Keeping the Pace

Anyone in their right mind who is participating in triathlons and Iron Man competitions enlists a partner to keep them motivated through the gruelling hours of training. For George Gollego, who became a paraplegic after tripping on a cable that had been carelessly left on the floor at his office two decades ago, that partner is his dog, Picasso.

After the accident, 'My life changed completely,' Gollego recalls. He went on to found Wheels in Progress, a group dedicated to helping young residents whose homes have become inaccessible to them because of spinal cord injuries. He also began racing to raise money for the cause. And he found Picasso.

The steady-moving dog encourages Gollego to stay on point, keeping him company through four- to six-hour training sessions. In 2011, Gollego completed the New York City Triathlon and raised enough money to move a 21-year-old from a residential nursing home into an apartment, all with the support of Picasso's companionship. 'How can a dog not be a man's best friend?' Gollego marvels. ▦

George Gollego trains with encouragement from his devoted companion in New York City's Central Park.

How To: Make a Whistle Out of an Acorn Cap

Communication is vital and in the wilderness even the simplest signal can save lives.

1 Find a hollowed-out acorn cap with a smooth interior and no holes or breaks.

2 Hold it between thumbs and forefingers, with thumbs forming a V shape on top.

3 Blow into the V space between your thumbs. Adjust slightly until you are able to make a sharp, shrill sound.

EXPERT TIP: While awaiting rescue, try to attract attention. Whistles are good audio signalling devices over short distances because high-pitched sounds are easier to pinpoint than low ones. After rescuers know your location, you can pass along more detailed information.

VISIONS OF EARTH

On Fourth Lake in New York's Adirondacks, a crush of 1,902 canoes and kayaks attempts to break a 'largest raft' world record.

Giant Sequoias Grow Faster with Age

Older trees beat youngsters when it comes to bulking up. Aging giant sequoia trees are growing faster than ever, with some of the oldest and tallest trees producing more wood, on average, in old age than they did when they were younger.

A 2,000-year-old giant sequoia is just cranking out wood, says Steve Sillett, a professor at Humboldt State University in California who has conducted recent research on the big trees. Other long-lived trees like coast redwoods and Australia's *Eucalyptus regnans* also show an increase in wood production during old age, according to an article Sillett published in the journal *Forest Ecology and Management.*

That may be because a tree's leaf area increases as its crown expands over a long life span. The leaves produce more sugars through photosynthesis and these sugars build wood across a growing cambium, the living surface separating bark and wood in trees. 'What we're finding,' says Sillett, 'is that the rate of wood production in some species doesn't slow down until a tree gets to the end of its lifetime.'

The old stumps don't rest; sequoias are active even in extreme old age. Sillett's team recently measured the President, a 3,200-year-old giant sequoia tree in California's Sequoia National Park. By climbing and measuring the tree, they calculated that the 75-metre-tall (247-foot) giant holds more than 1,500 cubic metres (54,000 cubic feet) of wood and bark, earning it the ranking of second largest tree on Earth, as reported in *National Geographic* magazine.

'Eventually every tree will suffer structural collapse and fall apart,' notes Sillett. 'All Earthlings have finite life spans, but some trees live more than a thousand years without slowing down.'

Sillett, a National Geographic explorer, is also co-leading the Redwoods and Climate Change Initiative group investigating how climate change may affect tree growth. They've established long-term monitoring plots throughout the geographic ranges of both California redwood species and have recorded growth histories of more than a hundred trees.

Because the trees are still alive, they can go back to specific trees and evaluate predictions about their growth responses to climate variation. 'Annual rings provide a wonderful, long-term record of a tree's performance,' Sillett says. 'By studying a tree's rings, we can, in a sense, translate what it knows about the forest.'

Cohabitation

A giant sequoia is an ecosystem unto itself. Most of its inhabitants are insects – from beetles to butterflies to wasps. All make good use of the sequoia's offerings. Bats roost in the foliage and under loose bark. Ample shade nurtures plants like the pink pygmy rose and the wildflower called little prince's pine.

A team of scientists measure a giant sequoia to determine its age and the amount of wood the tree contains in California's Sequoia National Park.

Perched on the tendril of a *Passiflora* plant, the egg of the Julia Heliconian butterfly may be safe from hungry ants.

Credit Cards

Several thousand years ago, the Babylonians extended credit by using clay tablets for barter transactions. An item and quantity would be marked, and the tablet could be redeemed for, say, two cows, or whatever was agreed upon. The Romans further developed the arts of borrowing and lending, and by the Middle Ages the concept of credit had come to include bills of exchange issued by banks. From the 17th to the 19th century, English tallymen sold goods on an installment plan, notching the transactions on a stick or 'tally.'

The first credit cards began appearing in Europe around the 1880s. These were essentially charge cards, allowing users to delay payment for a time (usually one month), after which the balance had to be paid—as opposed to today's credit cards, which can carry balances month to month. ▧

Grey Phalarope

Phalaropus fulicarius

LENGTH: 20–22 cm
WINGSPAN: 41–43 cm

This rare migrant spends winters at sea, but is occasionally sighted around the coast of the U.K. after a heavy north-east gale. Larger than the red-necked phalarope, the bird's voice is a simple *chit* in flight. It is one of the few species in which the more colourful female leaves the male to take care of the eggs and the young. ▧

Strange . . . But True: Time

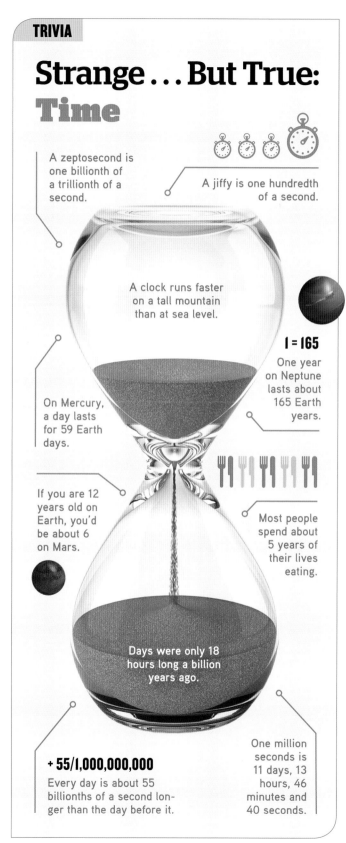

A zeptosecond is one billionth of a trillionth of a second.

A jiffy is one hundredth of a second.

A clock runs faster on a tall mountain than at sea level.

1 = 165
One year on Neptune lasts about 165 Earth years.

On Mercury, a day lasts for 59 Earth days.

If you are 12 years old on Earth, you'd be about 6 on Mars.

Most people spend about 5 years of their lives eating.

Days were only 18 hours long a billion years ago.

+ 55/1,000,000,000
Every day is about 55 billionths of a second longer than the day before it.

One million seconds is 11 days, 13 hours, 46 minutes and 40 seconds.

The fiery leaves of a gnarled and moss-covered Japanese maple make an arresting sight at the Portland Japanese Garden in Oregon.

NEVER YET WAS A SPRINGTIME / WHEN THE BUDS FORGOT TO BLOW

MAY

Istanbul, Turkey

Turkey's coast rivals the major Mediterranean resort destinations and boasts spectacular tourist attractions in the interior, including culture-rich Istanbul.

First Byzantium, then Constantinople during the Roman Empire and finally Istanbul during the Ottoman Empire – the name of the city may have changed over the centuries, but its allure and strategic importance astride the Bosporus have never waned. The jewel of Islamic art and architecture, its most famous highlights are the Galata Bridge over the Golden Horn; swarming crowds at the Grand Bazaar, the last stop on the Silk Road; the rare elegance of the 17th-century Sultan Ahmed Mosque (Blue Mosque), adorned with blue mosaics; and the Hagia Sophia, a 4th-century church transformed into a mosque and later a museum.

The country is astonishingly rich in archaeological sites, too. These include the ruins at Troy (which have only a distant tie to the legendary stories by Homer); Ephesus, a Greco-Roman city and one of the Seven Wonders of the Ancient World; and Aphrodisias, site of a Greco-Roman auditorium and stadium. ▥

Illuminated against a cerulean night sky, Istanbul's Blue Mosque represents the epitome of Ottoman art.

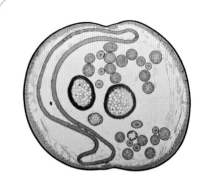

Killer Plants Strike via Underground Leaves

Why does a plant that survives on sunlight grow leaves beneath the earth? Flowering plants of the genus *Philcoxia* use subterranean leaves to trap tiny roundworms, or nematodes, that are vital for the plant's survival in the nutrient-deprived savannas of central Brazil – making these some of a mere 0.2 per cent of flowering plant species known to digest meat.

Apes Have Midlife Crises, Too

Too bad chimpanzees can't buy sports cars. New research says it's not just humans who go through midlife crises.

Chimpanzee
Pan troglodytes
SIZE: 1.2 – 1.7 m
WEIGHT: 32 – 60 kg
RANGE: Tropical forests of Africa

Chimps and orangutans, as well as humans, experience a dip in happiness around the middle of their lives. 'There may be different things going on at the surface, but underneath it all, there's something common in all three species that's leading to this,' says Alexander Weiss, a primate psychologist at the University of Edinburgh.

Weiss led a study team that asked long-term keepers of more than 500 chimpanzees and orangutans at zoos in five countries to evaluate the well-being of each animal they work with, including overall mood, how much the animals seemed to enjoy social interactions and how successful they were in achieving goals (such as obtaining a desired item).

When Weiss's team plotted the results on a graph, they saw a familiar curve, bottoming out in the middle of the animals' lives and rising again in old age. It's the same U-shape that has shown up in several studies about age and happiness in people, which usually reaches the lowest point between age 45 and 55.

Although the stereotype of a midlife crisis is generally negative, Weiss believes such ennui may have an evolutionary upside. By the middle of one's life, humans and apes often have access to more resources than when they were younger, which could make it easier to achieve goals. Discontentment, Weiss hypothesises, may be nature's way of motivating us to 'strike while the iron is hot.' ▥

Not so cheeky: new research suggests that chimps and orangutans can experience a midlife rut just as humans can.

STRANGE ... BUT TRUE! Yawns, thought to be a sign of empathy among species, are contagious for chimpanzees, just as they are for humans.

Without a Trace

A genetic mutation may be the first link in a long chain of events that starts in the womb and ultimately causes some people to be born without fingerprints, according to experts at the Tel Aviv Sourasky Medical Center.

Almost every person is born with fingerprints and everyone's are unique. But people with a rare disease known as adermatoglyphia lack fingerprints from birth. Affecting only four known extended families worldwide, the condition is also called 'immigration-delay disease', since a lack of fingerprints makes it difficult for people to cross international borders.

In an effort to find the cause of the disease, dermatologist Eli Sprecher sequenced the DNA of 16 members of one family with adermatoglyphia in Switzerland. Seven had normal fingerprints and the other nine did not. After investigating a number of genes to find evidence of mutation, the researchers came up empty-handed – until a grad student finally found the culprit, a smaller version of a gene designated SMARCAD1.

The larger SMARCAD1 is expressed throughout the body, but the smaller form acts only on the skin. Sure enough, the nine family members with no fingerprints had mutations in that gene. Being born without fingerprints doesn't occur simply because one gene has been turned on or off, Sprecher observes. Rather, the mutation causes copies of the SMARCAD1 gene to be unstable.

Other inherited diseases that result in a lack of fingerprints – such as Naegeli syndrome – are caused by problems with the protein keratin-14. Unlike immigration-delay disease, whose only known side effect is a minor reduction in the ability to sweat, these conditions manifest with other features like the thickening of skin and problems with nail formation.

Through further study of the Swiss family, Sprecher believes, it might be possible to solve the mystery of fingerprints overall. 'You go from a rare disease to a biological insight of general importance,' he says. 'We would never have been able to get to this gene if not for the study of this family.'

Vanishing Act Children's less oily fingerprints disappear from surfaces faster than adults' do.

Arava the tortoise and her new set of wheels. To the bemusement of the other tortoises, Arava can now zip around her enclosure.

Arava:
The Tortoise Wins Again

No one expects tortoises to be speed demons. But when Arava, an African spurred tortoise, got a 'skateboard' for her back legs, she became speedier than most.

Arava had arrived at the Jerusalem Biblical Zoo unable to move her hind legs. 'She wouldn't eat and tucked her head inside her shell,' recalls veterinarian Nili Avni-Magen. 'She seemed so sad.' The medical staff couldn't find a reason for the paralysis, but they had a solution: wheels.

Arava could still use her front legs, so a metalworker built a two-wheeled metal platform with straps to go around Arava's shell. When Arava first tried out her skateboard, she took a few steps with her front legs and started rolling. Now she zips around her enclosure on her board, outrunning the other tortoises. Arava has a long life to look forward to – unless she tries to ollie out of a ramp. ▥

How To: Make a Shadow Stick

No compass? No problem. The universe contains its own direction-finding aid: the sun.

1 Use a pebble to mark the tip of a vertical stick's shadow in the morning.

2 With a string tied to the stick's base, draw a circle on the ground around the stick, using the pebble as a point on the arc and the stick as centre.

3 As the sun ascends, the stick's shadow shrinks. Then, after midday, the shadow lengthens again. With another pebble, mark the spot where the growing shadow first touches the arc in the afternoon. Now the two pebbles, widely spaced, form an east–west line. West is marked by the first pebble.

EXPERT TIP: Shadows cast at noon point north in the northern hemisphere and south in the southern hemisphere. Heat and light from the south (in the northern hemisphere) also affect plant growth, which can be examined for directional clues on cloudy days.

In a sunlit courtyard in Mandalay, Myanmar, four young monks enjoy some time off with a game of football.

A New Norse Legacy

For the past 50 years – since the discovery of a thousand-year-old Viking way station in Newfoundland – archaeologists and amateur historians have combed North America's east coast searching for traces of Viking visitors.

It has been a long, fruitless quest, spanning more than a decade and littered with bizarre claims and embarrassing failures. But at a conference in Canada in October 2012, archaeologist Patricia Sutherland announced new evidence that points strongly to the discovery of the second Viking outpost ever discovered in the Americas.

While digging in the ruins of a centuries-old building on Baffin Island, far above the Arctic Circle, a team led by Sutherland, adjunct professor of archaeology at Memorial University in Newfoundland and a research fellow at the University of Aberdeen in Scotland, found some very intriguing whetstones. Wear grooves in the blade-sharpening tools bear traces of copper alloys such as bronze – materials known to have been made by Viking metalsmiths but unknown among the Arctic's native inhabitants.

Taken together with her earlier discoveries, Sutherland's new findings strengthen the case for a Viking camp on Baffin Island. Archaeologists have long known that Viking seafarers set sail for the New World around A.D. 1000. A popular Icelandic saga tells of the exploits of Leif Eriksson, a Viking chieftain from Greenland who sailed westward to seek his fortune. According to the saga, Eriksson stopped long enough on Baffin Island to walk the coast – named Helluland, an Old Norse word meaning 'stone-slab land' – before heading south.

Sutherland speculates that parties of Viking seafarers travelled to the Canadian Arctic to search for valuable resources. In northern Europe at the time, medieval nobles prized walrus ivory, soft Arctic furs and other northern luxuries – and Dorset hunters and trappers could readily stockpile such products. Helluland's waters teemed with walruses and its coasts abounded in Arctic foxes and other small fur-bearing animals. To barter for such goods Viking traders likely offered bits of iron and wood that could be carved into figurines and other goods.

If Sutherland is correct, the lines of evidence she has uncovered may point to a previously unknown chapter in New World history in which Viking seafarers and Native American hunters were partners in a transatlantic trade network. 'I think things were a lot more complex in this part of the world than most people assumed,' Sutherland says. ▮

Metallurgy Unlocks the Mystery
Using a technique known as energy dispersive spectroscopy to examine the wear grooves on more than 20 whetstones from Tanfield and other sites, Sutherland detected microscopic streaks of bronze, brass and iron – believed to be evidence of European metallurgy.

This ancient life-size mask was used in Shamanic rituals, during which participants would strive to reach altered states of consciousness and connect with the spirit world.

A magnificent firework
display lights up the night
sky over the gardens
of Vaux-le-Vicomte in
Maincy, France.

Chess

One of the oldest board games still being played, chess is believed to have its origins in a Hindustani game called *chaturanga* played in the sixth century A.D. or earlier in India and Persia. The name refers to the four parts of the army – elephants, horses, chariots (or boats) and foot soldiers.

By the time it was introduced to the West in the seventh or eighth century, it had more or less taken on the format known today – a two-player game, each with 16 pieces that are moved, according to type, across a 64-square board to checkmate (capture) the opponent's king. Muslims took the game of chess to Spain, the Byzantines brought it to Italy and by the year 1000 it had spread throughout Europe, finding great popularity with the aristocracy. ▦

Eurasian Hoopoe

Upupa epops

LENGTH: 26–28 cm
WINGSPAN: 42–46 cm

A highly distinctive, hollow *poo-poo-poo*, much like the sound of air being blown into a bottle, is the mating call of this broad-winged bird. When agitated, however, it lets out a harsh Eurasian jay-like *schaar*. The hoopoe favours dry or fairly dry lands, in both cultivated and uncultivated areas with trees and bushes. ▦

Strange...But True:
Speed

.007 KPH

Some avalanches travel more than 160 kilometres an hour (100 mph).

Elephants can run faster than humans.

A snail would take about 136 hours to crawl 1.6 kilometres (1 mile) nonstop.

Light travels faster than sound.

If you travelled at the speed of light, you could reach Pluto in just 4 hours.

A hippo can run as fast as a human.

A swordfish can swim about as fast as a cheetah can run.

When you see lightning, it's travelling at about 365 million kilometres an hour (227 million mph).

A lone loggerhead turtle
paddles through the crystalline
waters of Palm Beach, Florida.

AND THE LANDSCAPE / LAY AS IF NEW-CREATED IN ALL THE FRESHNESS OF CHILDHOOD

JUNE

Rio de Janeiro, Brazil

Brazil's capital, Rio de Janeiro, is a city of glitz and glamour and an electric sports scene will add to its universal allure when the football World Cup comes in 2014.

Pure magic as seen from Pão de Açúcar (Sugarloaf): water, sky, landscape and lights converge into a breathtaking panorama.

Fantastic Voyage

A study of *Tornatellides boeningi* – a snail common on Hahajima Island about 100 kilometres (620 miles) south of Tokyo – revealed that as many as 15 per cent of the tiny gastropods are able to survive being eaten by certain bird species. What's more, the surviving snails remained healthy; one even gave birth shortly after emerging from the 30-minute to 2-hour digestion process.

'Marvellous city, full of a thousand charms,' sang Aurora Miranda in a 1934 Carnival hit that's now Rio de Janeiro's anthem. To put this song to the test, each year as many people visit Rio as live there – riding cable cars up to Pão de Açúcar and trams through Santa Teresa; going inside belle epoque palaces at Cinelândia and pleasure palaces at Copacabana; climbing to the Rocinha favela (shantytown) by minibus; shouting samba lyrics at the Sambódromo parade grounds and, of course, 'Go!' at Maracanã football stadium.

Officially known as the Estadio Jornalista Mario Filho, the Marcanã stadium was built for the 1950 FIFA World Cup Brazil. In the summer, the colossal arena will host up to seven games of the 2014 World Cup. Do as the *cariocas* (Rio natives) do and show your unbridled enthusiasm at one of the spirited sporting events. Rio has a pace all its own and *cariocas* are known for enjoying life. ▥

Waste Wattage: Riding the Sustainability Wave

Shower drains and dirty dishwater and laundry water could be on the cutting edge of energy efficiency and recovery.

Around the world, cities are realising that the water leaving our homes and offices – specifically, warm and hot wastewater – is an astoundingly powerful source of energy.

The technology is simple. Wastewater, which consists of what gets flushed down toilets but is mixed with millions of litres of hot water from showers, dishwashers, washing machines and more, maintains a fairly constant temperature as it travels through sewers to the treatment plant – typically about 15°C (59°F), though this varies by geography and season. In a sewage heat recovery system, a heat pump is used to capture the warmth of wastewater and transfer it to the clean water stream that is entering homes and businesses. It all operates as a closed-loop system, of course, meaning that the dirty water never touches the clean water. But the warmth of the sewage water helps heat the water that is used in appliances, including radiators, to help heat buildings.

The trick of the system is that it takes a lot less energy to heat 15°C water than to heat ice-cold water. And in the summer, buildings with sewage heat recovery systems can reverse their heat pumps and use the 15°C sewage to dissipate excess building heat and reduce a building's air-conditioning costs. By utilising piping that's already in place, the 'sewer thermal' method offers a nonintrusive, cost-effective means of conservation. ▦

Cities like Vancouver in Canada are beginning to harness the power of wastewater as an energy-saving mechanism.

STRANGE...BUT TRUE! It takes 2,700 litres (713 gallons) of water – the amount the average person consumes in three years – to make one cotton T-shirt.

How the Nose Knows

Millions of receptors in the nose's smelling organ aren't scattered at random. Instead, the receptors congregate in small regions that help the brain discern good smells from bad ones, among other potential functions.

Researchers gathered evidence by sticking electronic probes up people's noses and measuring the chatter of nasal neurons as subjects were exposed to scents. Their findings imply that the pleasantness of a smell is hardwired within our heads, calling into question the impact of life experience on how people perceive smells.

'It's both exciting and disturbing,' says Don Wilson of the New York University School of Medicine, a neurobiologist who was not involved in the work. 'It doesn't fit in with what I think or a lot of other researchers think about smell.' Instead of the brain processing all scent information, for instance, it seems nasal neurons preprocess some of it – almost as if the nose has its own small brain.

The human nose contains a postage stamp–sized smelling organ, called the olfactory epithelium, at the roof of the nasal cavity. By probing mouse noses to measure the firing of nasal neurons, scientists had previously discovered that scent receptors might be organised into groups, similar to the way the tongue has zones armed to detect specific tastes such as sour, sweet and salty.

According to another study led by neuroscientist Noam Sobel of the Weizmann Institute of Science in Israel, in which the team pooled together 801 neurological recordings from more than 80 people's noses, some regions of the epithelium are better at detecting scent than other regions. The researchers also found hot spots that are better at interpreting pleasantness and unpleasantness. The precise purpose of the programmed zones, however, remains a subject of study. ▦

Super Sense
Only three receptor types facilitate colour vision, but roughly 400 kinds of receptors contribute to human smell.

Ricochet:
Putting the 'Surf' in Service

Ricochet was bred to be a service dog, but her owner, Judy Fridono, was having trouble motivating the golden retriever. The only thing Ricochet seemed to enjoy was balancing on a surfboard in a paddling pool, an activity used to help hone service dogs' coordination. So, when Fridono heard about a nearby dog surfing competition, she entered it on a whim. Ricochet stunned everyone by winning third place.

Determined to find a way for Ricochet to give back with her skill, Fridono decided the dog could help raise money for charity. She contacted another surfer, Patrick Ivison, an acquaintance who is a quadriplegic. The two planned an event where the boy and dog would surf side by side to help pay for Ivison's physical therapy. The event raised $10,000 and set in motion a booming fundraising career for Ricochet, who can be seen hanging ten on numerous YouTube videos today.

Ricochet the amazing surf dog shares a board with Patrick Ivison. Ricochet's skill helps pay for Ivison's physical therapy.

How To: Collect Water From Dew

A basic resource, water is everywhere in the temperate forest – not just in rivers and lakes.

1 Wrap your legs with clean clothes or towels and tie them in place. If you have no clean clothes, choose the least dirty ones – probably shirts since they are less in contact with the ground than trousers or socks.

2 Walk through shrubs and tall grass around sunrise, when dew forms, until the clothes or towels are saturated. Squeeze out the water into a container or suck it out of the fabric directly. Dew, a pure form of water as it condenses out of the atmosphere, is drinkable unless it forms on a contaminated surface. Be sure to collect dew early in the morning before it evaporates.

EXPERT TIP: Look for ways to get water out of air, soil and living tissue. Collecting rain on a tarp, gathering snow below its surface, digging into soil for groundwater and extracting drinkable liquid from fish are all options.

The crackle of fireworks, believed to bring good fortune, heralds the yearly Dragon Boat Festival in China's Guangzhou province.

The Secret (Chinese) Ingredients of (Almost) Everything

Most of us would be hard-pressed to locate Inner Mongolia, Jiangxi or Guangdong on a map. Yet many of the high-tech devices we depend on – mobile phones and laptops among others – would not exist without an obscure group of elements mined in these areas.

Rare earths, as the elements are called, were discovered in the late 18th century as oxidised minerals – hence 'earths'. They're actually metals and they aren't really rare; they're just scattered. A handful of dirt from your backyard would probably contain a smidgen, maybe a few parts per million. The rarest rare earth is nearly 200 times more abundant than gold. But deposits large and concentrated enough to be worth mining are indeed rare.

China, which supplies 97 per cent of the world's rare earth needs, rattled global markets in the autumn of 2010 when it cut off shipments to Japan for a month during a diplomatic dispute. Over the next decade, China is expected to steadily reduce rare earth exports in order to protect the supplies of its own rapidly growing industries, which already consume about 60 per cent of the rare earths produced in the country. Fears of future shortages have sent prices soaring.

The demand shows no signs of abating, either. In 2015, the world's industries are forecast to consume an estimated 185,000 tons of rare earths, 50 per cent more than the total for 2010. So with China holding tightly to its reserves, where will the rest of the world get the elements that have become so vital to modern technology?

American dominance of the market ended in the mid-1980s. China, which for decades had been developing the technology for separating rare earths (not easy to do because they're chemically so similar), stepped onto the scene with a roar. With government support, cheap labour and lax or nonexistent environmental regulations, its rare earth industries undercut all competitors. The Mountain Pass mine in California closed in 2002 and Baotou, a city in Inner Mongolia (an autonomous region of China), became the world's new rare earth capital.

Baotou has paid a steep price for its supremacy. Nearby villagers reportedly have been relocated because their water and crops have been contaminated with mining wastes. Furthermore, smaller mines in southern China often operate outside of the law, run by violent criminal gangs with little regard for environmental protection. The situation is not sustainable, but with digital devices ever on the rise, the world will continue scrambling to find sources of these precious elements. ∎

> 'They're all around you. They're hidden unless you know about them.'
> –karlgschneidner, metallurgist

Rare earths help MP3 players
and phones emit sound and light.
Neodymium magnets animate
the speaker, the vibrating motor
and the tiny earbuds.

A cluster of high-rises jostle for space in Hong Kong's Kowloon district, one of the most densely populated areas in the world.

Bicycle

The first bicycle-like vehicle was the creation of German engineer Baron Karl von Drais. His 1817 *draisienne* looked much like a modern bicycle, minus pedals. The wooden machine was propelled by the rider's feet.

A much better bicycle came along in 1861, the product of French father and son Pierre and Ernest Michaux. Their *vélocipède* had pedals attached to a large front wheel made of iron or solid rubber – which made for such a bumpy ride that it was nicknamed the 'boneshaker'. In England, a similar contraption became known as the penny farthing (after the penny coin and the much smaller farthing), its front wheel as large as a metre and a half (5 feet) in diameter. In 1885, the safety bicycle was introduced by English bicyclemaker J. K. Starley. ▥

Common Cuckoo

Cuculus canorus

LENGTH: 32–34 cm
WINGSPAN: 55–60 cm

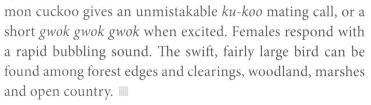

One of the most widespread and best-known species of Europe, the common cuckoo gives an unmistakable *ku-koo* mating call, or a short *gwok gwok gwok* when excited. Females respond with a rapid bubbling sound. The swift, fairly large bird can be found among forest edges and clearings, woodland, marshes and open country. ▥

Strange . . . But True: Senses

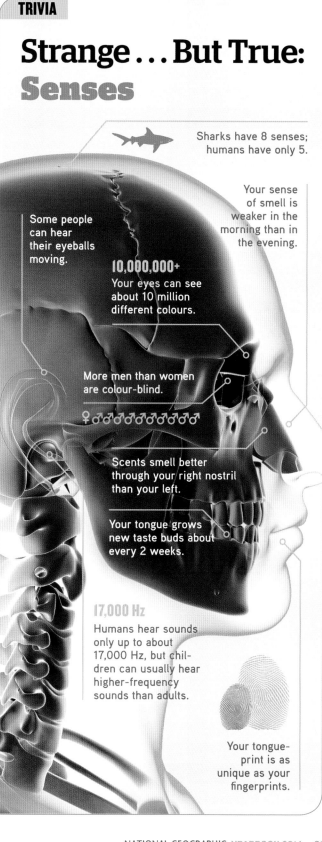

Sharks have 8 senses; humans have only 5.

Some people can hear their eyeballs moving.

Your sense of smell is weaker in the morning than in the evening.

10,000,000+
Your eyes can see about 10 million different colours.

More men than women are colour-blind.

Scents smell better through your right nostril than your left.

Your tongue grows new taste buds about every 2 weeks.

17,000 Hz
Humans hear sounds only up to about 17,000 Hz, but children can usually hear higher-frequency sounds than adults.

Your tongue-print is as unique as your fingerprints.

A swimmer ducks below a breaking wave in the powerful surf at Coogee Beach in Sydney, Australia.

HOT JULY BRINGS COOLING SHOWERS, / APRICOTS AND GILLYFLOWERS

JULY

St. Petersburg, Russia

When the sun lights St. Petersburg for more than 20 hours a day in the summertime, the atmosphere is Bacchanalian and the panoramas and silhouettes are second to none.

Peter the Great's stately Baltic city built on 42 Neva delta islands celebrates 'white nights' (near round-the-clock summer sunlight) with joyful abandon. From late May to mid-July, the skies above St. Petersburg's Peter and Paul Fortress (the resting place of the tsars) and Nevsky Prospekt (the city's main thoroughfare) glow pale blue, pink and peach well after midnight. Cruise the canals and River Neva on a guided White Nights boat tour and then stroll atop the Neva Embankments – elegant granite barriers built to control flooding – to watch the four illuminated Neva drawbridges open at around 2 a.m.

In addition to the drawbridges, Nevsky Prospekt is accessible by five metro stations, all leading to the 4.5-kilometre (3-mile) stretch of shops, restaurants, grand palaces, museums and cathedrals. Exploring on foot is recommended. The city is ripe with attractions and the straight streets are dissected by waterways, making it difficult to get lost. ▨

Known as the 'Venice of the North,' St. Petersburg is built on dozens of small islands on the Neva River and along canals.

Prehistoric Provisions

Buried under the seabed for 86 million years, a bacterial community lives so slowly, according to a new study, that it's still surviving on an organic carbon 'lunch box' from the dino era. It's been known since the 1990s that microbes can live trapped in ocean sediments for millions of years, but scientists are just beginning to understand how the mud-dwelling bacteria sustains itself.

Are Honeybees Losing Their Way?

Honeybee
Apis mellifera
SIZE: 1 – 1.5 cm
WEIGHT: 90 mg +
RANGE: Worldwide distribution

A single honeybee visits hundreds, sometimes thousands, of flowers a day, crossing great distances in search of nectar and pollen before it must navigate back to the hive.

A new study published in the *Journal of Experimental Biology*, however, shows that long-term exposure to a combination of certain pesticides might impede the bee's ability to carry out its pollen mission. 'Any impairment in their ability to do this could have a strong effect on their survival,' notes Geraldine Wright, a neuroscientist at Newcastle University and co-author of the 2013 study.

Wright's work adds to the growing body of research that shows that the honeybee's ability to thrive is being threatened. A rapid die-off known as colony collapse disorder (CCD) has been observed in millions of honeybees throughout the world since 2006. Scientists are still researching how pesticides may be contributing to this problem, but in Wright's estimation, 'Pesticides are very likely to be involved in CCD and also in the loss of other types of pollinators.'

Bees depend on what's called 'scent memory' to find flowers teeming with nectar and pollen. Their ability to rapidly learn, remember and communicate with each other has made them highly efficient foragers, using a clever choreographed dance to educate others about the site of the food source. The bees' speed and orientation during the telltale waggle dance, which follows a figure-eight motion, indicate the direction of the flowers in relation to the sun, the distance and the flower type. ▓

A European honeybee pollinates a flower. Scientists are concerned that exposure to pesticides is impairing the bees' navigational abilities.

STRANGE . . . BUT TRUE! When a queen bee dies, workers create a new queen by feeding a worker female a special diet of 'royal jelly' which enhances fertility.

Mystery Solved: Why We Sunburn

New research suggests that sun exposure may set off chemical 'alarms' in our cells, triggering inflammation.

'Sunburn is a common experience for human beings,' says Richard L. Gallo, professor of medicine and chief of dermatology at the University of California, San Diego, School of Medicine, yet 'there's surprisingly little information on how energy in sunlight is detected [in the body] as a source of danger.'

Gallo's team has identified the chemical culprit that triggers our skin's warning signs. A type of RNA, they found it breaks into pieces within a dead cell destroyed by ultraviolet sunlight. Next, so-called receptor molecules in neighbouring cells detect the damaged RNA and tell the body to inflame the healthy skin around the dead cell – voilà, sunburn.

Usually, RNA acts as a messenger in our bodies, 'coding' DNA, with which RNA shares its double-helix structure. But the kind of RNA that triggers sunburn is called noncoding RNA – it doesn't transmit genetic information, but instead controls how our genes work. Testing suggests that a type of receptor that normally detects foreign RNA in viruses also recognises the broken RNA within sun-damaged cells and subsequently triggers the inflammation process.

Inflammation can be beneficial for several reasons, Gallo notes. For starters, it removes sun-zapped cells, allowing the skin to heal. The team also suspects the inflammatory process may clear out cells with genetic damage before they can become cancerous. And, of course, sunburn is unpleasant – the inflammation 'teaches us that getting that sunlight is not such a good thing,' says Gallo.

Understanding how sunburn happens may help scientists develop inflammation blockers, which could potentially benefit people with autoimmune diseases that result in high sun sensitivity, such as lupus. ▓

Joe:
Redefining Table Etiquette

Joe the Bactrian camel is much too fancy to have breakfast in his stable. Instead, the fine diner eats morning meals with his keepers at the kitchen table in their home in Ashbourne, Derbyshire.

'The first time Joe showed up for a bite, we definitely weren't expecting him,' says owner Nathan Anderson-Dixon. The animal had been grazing in his pasture when he smelled food cooking. Following his nose, he trotted up to the house through an unlocked gate, poked his head into an open kitchen window and gently plucked a morsel of food from the table with his lips.

Now Joe is a regular visitor at breakfast. His favourite treats are cereal and toast topped with bananas. At first, his owners weren't sure they wanted the humped guest dining with them. But they've grown fond of his daily appearances. 'Joe's a member of the family,' Anderson-Dixon says. If only he'd learn to use a napkin. ▓

Joe the camel joins the Anderson-Dixon family for breakfast each morning via an open window in their farmhouse's kitchen.

How To: Improvise Sunglasses

The sun serves as a useful guiding tool, but too much of anything can be hazardous.

1 Slice a piece of cloth, leather, tree bark or something similar to fit over the eyes like a mask.

2 Cut narrow horizontal slits for each eye. Make sure they're big enough to see out of, yet let in as little light as possible.

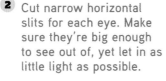

3 Apply soot under your eyes to reduce glare. The sun's ultraviolet light, reflecting off sand or light-coloured rocks, can burn the surface of the eyes from below.

4 Tie the mask in place with a string or cord.

EXPERT TIP: When packing, take two pairs of sunglasses in case one breaks. Consider wearing fabrics specially made to absorb ultraviolet radiation, designated by a UPF (ultraviolet protection factor) rating.

VISIONS OF EARTH

Recently retired from use in logging, an Asian elephant makes its way through a sunlit forest on Havelock Island of the Andaman Islands in India.

Pyramid Puzzle: Cracking an Old Case

A sealed space in Egypt's Great Pyramid may help solve a centuries-old mystery: how did the ancient Egyptians move two million 2.5-ton blocks to build the ancient wonder?

A little-known cavity in the 4,500-year-old monument to Pharaoh Khufu may support the theory that the pyramid was constructed inside out, via a spiralling, inclined interior tunnel – an idea that contradicts the prevailing wisdom that the monuments were built using an external ramp. The inside-out theory's key proponent, French architect Jean-Pierre Houdin, says that for centuries Egyptologists have ignored evidence staring them in the face. 'The paradigm was wrong,' Houdin insists. 'The idea that the pyramids were built from the outside was just wrong.'

Houdin's theory suggests the Great Pyramid was built in two stages. First, he believes, blocks were hauled up a straight external ramp to build the pyramid's bottom third, which contains most of the monument's mass. Houdin adds that the limestone blocks used in the outside ramp were recycled for the pyramid's upper levels, which would explain why no trace of an original ramp has been found. After the foundation was finished, Houdin says, workers began building an inclined, internal, corkscrew tunnel, which would continue its path up and around as the pyramid rose.

New evidence uncovered about two-thirds of the way up the Great Pyramid might support the inside-out theory. At about the 90-metre (300-foot) mark on the north-eastern edge lies an open notch leading into a small L-shaped room. For the interior tunnel to work, it would have required open areas at the Great Pyramid's four corners. Otherwise the blocks wouldn't have been able to clear the 90-degree turns. Like railroad roundhouses, these open corners would have given workers room to pivot the blocks – perhaps using wooden cranes – so the stones could be pushed into the next tunnel.

This notch and room are remnants of one such opening, Houdin claims. They are located at one of the spots where Houdin's 3-D computer models suggest they should be. Inside the corner space, which was apparently walled in as the pyramid was completed, there should be two tunnel entrances at right angles to each other – each leading to a section of the internal ramp, Houdin believes. Perhaps all that stands between him and the solution to the mystery are massive blocks that thousands of years ago sealed the tunnel. ▪

Stone Cold Facts
The Great Pyramid is estimated to have about 2,300,000 stone blocks, the heaviest of which are believed to weigh as much as 70 tons. There are no hieroglyphics or writing on the stones in the pyramid.

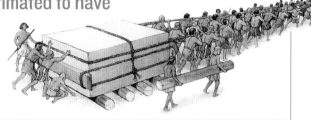

The Great Pyramid at Giza is the only wonder of the ancient world that still exists, but scientists are still not clear as to how it was built

EDITOR'S PICK

An arctic fox steals a snow goose egg on Wrangel Island, a protected nature sanctuary in the Arctic Ocean.

Ice Cream

Ice cream's early history is spotty: some ancient civilizations knew about freezing foods and some of the first iced 'creams' (including the snow and syrup enjoyed by Emperor Nero in the first century A.D.) would resemble sorbets to modern palates. King Charles I of England in the 17th century offered his chef a lifetime pension for keeping an 'iced cream' recipe secret.

By the 18th century, recipes for ice cream as we understand it appeared in British and American cookbooks. Advances in commercial refrigeration really paved the way for modern ice cream consumption; when large freezers became available, especially in transport, merchants could start offering different types, all the time. Today ice cream is available in hard and soft varieties, in flavours as diverse as garlic and basil and in cones, sandwiches and many other forms. ▤

BIRD OF THE MONTH

Willow Warbler

Phylloscopus trochilus

LENGTH: 11–13 cm
WINGSPAN: 18–20 cm

Common in a wide variety of woodlands and scrub, this species makes a soft *hooeet* with rising inflection, comparable to the call of western races of the similar-looking chiffchaff. The willow warbler's distinctive song is a series of delicate *swee* notes gradually increasing in volume before slowly descending in scale. ▤

TRIVIA

Strange ... But True: Technology

The world's first handheld mobile phone cost £2,644.

The first telephone answering machine was 90 cm (3 ft) tall.

There are more text messages sent each day than there are people on Earth.

The average computer user blinks 4 to 5 times per minute, less than half the normal rate of 12 to 15 blinks.

The world's fastest typist can reach speeds of 200 words per minute.

The first email was sent in 1971.

There are about a trillion Web pages on the Internet – that's about 140 for every person on Earth!

In Malaysia, people text 'HA3' instead of LOL.

Most of today's calculators are more powerful than the world's first computer.

Samburu families celebrate during a three-day wedding ceremony in Maralal, Kenya. The elaborate festivities are designed to ward off superstitions and bring good luck.

IN SUMMER THE SONG / SINGS ITSELF

AUGUST

Maasai-Mara National Reserve, Kenya

Kenya is the place for a great safari adventure for photographers and observers alike, but it also has wonderful beaches.

Kenya's fauna is remarkable. The 'big five' – elephants, lions, leopards, rhinos and cape buffalo – can be found here and are the main attractions for a photo safari. Visitors watch the animals from open Land Rovers poised for the perfect angle.

The big five come together in Maasai-Mara National Reserve, the most interesting and best known park. Hippopotamuses lounge in the Mara River and endless herds of gnus and zebras pass by in July and August during the great migration. Lake Nakuru harbours flamingo colonies and pelicans side by side with giraffes, gazelles and black rhinos.

While parks and reserves beckon inland, the Kenyan shores of the Indian Ocean have their own allure, with white sandy beaches, coconut palms and, above all, coral reefs where marine life can be studied at leisure. Diving, windsurfing and deep-sea fishing (especially for barracuda, marlin and tuna) are in fashion. So far, mass tourism hasn't reached these shores, but new resorts are springing up in areas like Shanzu and Chale Island. ▪

For these young lions of the Rekero pride in Kenya's Maasai-Mara National Reserve, tourists are a part of everyday life.

Seawater With a Kick

The elevated caffeine levels of the United States' Pacific Northwest don't stop at the shoreline; a new study finds that contaminants in human waste are entering natural water systems. Caffeine has been documented in waters around the world, including in the Mediterranean and the North Sea, but the stimulant's impact on the surrounding ecosystem is yet unknown.

A Golden Age for the Darling Guinea Pig

Guinea Pig
Cavia porcellus
SIZE: 19.8 – 50 cm
WEIGHT: 0.5 – 1.5 kg
RANGE: Northwestern Venezuela to central Chile

When Spanish conquistadores brought guinea pigs from South America to Europe, the tiny 'curiosities' were bred as pets across a wide swath of Elizabethan societal classes.

The evidence comes from a guinea pig skeleton discovered in 2007 in the cellar of a former middle-class house in Mons, Belgium, which was once part of the Spanish Empire. Radiocarbon dating of the bones revealed that this guinea pig lived between the end of the 16th and the beginning of the 17th centuries – very soon after the Spanish arrived in South America, reports study leader Fabienne Pigière of the Royal Belgian Institute of Natural Sciences in Brussels.

Guinea pig bones are rare in the European archaeological record, which left scientists wondering what purpose the animals originally served when they arrived on the continent. The new study suggests that early guinea pigs provided more companionship than sustenance. The Belgian guinea pig skeleton was found complete and without any evidence of being processed as food, so the authors are confident that the animal had been part of the family.

Guinea pigs have long been dinner in South America, but evidence suggests they were kept as family pets in the 16th-century in Europe.

But Elizabeth Reitz, a zooarchaeologist at the University of Georgia in Athens, notes that she wouldn't be surprised if Europeans ate guinea pigs, too – the English at the time regularly ate dormice. In fact, Pigière and colleagues found one historical reference that Europeans ate guinea pigs in a 1563 book written by French agronomist Olivier de Serres. De Serres wrote that it was 'necessary to have some spices to improve the flavour of guinea pig meat.' ▮

STRANGE . . . BUT TRUE!

Chimpanzees, monkeys, dogs, mice and a guinea pig have all journeyed into space.

RUSSIAN 1ST SPACEMAN

Maths Can Be Truly Painful

Does the thought of 1+1 equal ouch? Well, if you hate maths, it might – literally. According to a new study, the mere prospect of a maths problem causes pain centres to light up in number-phobic brains.

Researchers at the University of Chicago measured the neural activity of 28 adults – 14 who'd been identified with high maths anxiety and 14 with low maths anxiety. Each subject was given a series of word and maths tasks while his or her brain was scanned.

Result: When those in the high-anxiety group saw a maths task was coming, their dorso-posterior insulas and mid-cingulate cortices – the parts of the brain that perceive pain and bodily threats – reacted as if the subject's hand had been burned on a hot stove. Those in the low-anxiety group showed no such response.

What's more, said study co-author Ian Lyons, 'the anxiety occurred only during anticipation. When they actually did the math problems, they didn't seem to experience pain. That suggests it's not the math itself that hurts; it's the *thought* of it that's painful.' Previous studies have shown that psychologically stressful events – like the end of a romantic relationship – can cause physical discomfort. This study, published by Lyons and co-author Sian Beilock in the journal *PLoS One,* may be the first to show that anticipation alone can register in the brain as pain.

Can anything quell a maths hater's brain pain? 'The initial step is to get over the anxiety,' Lyons advises. And this is one case where practice doesn't make perfect. 'If you're math-anxious, just doing piles of math homework isn't a good idea. But finding a way to be more comfortable with the idea of math is.'

Effie:
Sniffing Out Disease

When Lisa Hulber took in homeless Effie, the situation didn't seem promising. 'She had every parasite known to dogdom,' says Hulber. 'She was really unadoptable.' But Hulber fell in love with her and rescued her anyway.

Four months after Hulber had a routine mammogram with normal results, Effie began repeatedly sticking her nose into Hulber's breast. 'I would push her away and she'd keep doing it,' Hulber remembers. Concerned, Hulber went back for another mammogram; again, it came back normal. Still convinced something was off, she went for an ultrasound and the doctor found a large carcinoma that rarely shows up on mammograms.

Hulber scheduled a mastectomy for a month later, during which time Effie began sniffing under her arm. Hulber showed the doctor the spot Effie had fixated on and when she awoke from surgery she was informed that Effie had been right. 'Of 27 lymph nodes, that was the only node it had spread to,' she says. 'A lot of women cry about losing their breasts, but what makes me cry is the gift this dog gave me.' ▦

When Lisa Hulber took in stray Effie, she never imagined her newfound friend would one day save her life.

How To: Make an Anti-Rodent Bag

Packing food is a necessity for longer trips, but unprotected rations are an open invitation for pests.

1 Secure food in an airtight or sturdy bag. The less porous the bag material, the better. You will also need a cord and a wide can.

2 Tie the cord to the bag and knot it well above the bag.

3 Punch a hole in a wide can and slide it down the cord until it stops at the knot. If the knot slips through the hole, tie the knot multiple times until it is big enough to stop the can.

4 Hang the bag several feet off the ground. The can acts as a barrier to prevent rodents from climbing down the cord.

EXPERT TIP: Fresh foods are refreshing and nutritious, but heat spoils them quickly. Be especially careful with fresh fruit, dairy products and meat. Travellers can avoid spoilage by packing dehydrated and freeze-dried foods.

VISIONS OF EARTH

On a hot summer's day in Waikiki, Hawaii, children await the perfect wave before plunging into the refreshing water below.

The Space-Weather Forecast

Few objects seem as familiar as the sun – there it is, up in the sky every sunny day – yet few are so strange. With a period of maximum solar activity expected this year, space-weather centres are adding staff to monitor the massive star.

On Thursday 1 September 1859, a 33-year-old amateur astronomer named Richard Carrington climbed the stairs to his private observatory near London, opened the dome slit and adjusted his telescope to project a 28-centimetre (11-inch) image of the sun onto a screen. He was tracing sunspots on a piece of paper when, before his eyes, 'two patches of intensely bright and white light' suddenly appeared amid one large sunspot group. At the same time, the magnetometer needle at London's Kew Observatory began dancing wildly. Before dawn the next day, enormous auroral displays of red, green and purple illuminated the skies as far south as Hawaii and Panama. Campers in the Rocky Mountains, mistaking the aurora for sunrise, got up and started cooking breakfast.

The flare Carrington had observed heralded a solar superstorm – an enormous electromagnetic outburst that sent billions of tons of charged particles hurtling toward Earth. When the invisible wave collided with the planet's magnetic field, it caused electrical currents to surge through telegraph lines. The blast knocked out service at several stations, but telegraphers elsewhere found that they could disconnect their batteries and resume operations using the geomagnetic electricity alone.

Operators of today's communication systems and power grids would be less sanguine. No solar superstorm as powerful as the 1859 event has occurred since, so it is difficult to calculate what impact a comparable storm might have on today's more wired world.

'We cannot predict what the sun will do more than a few days ahead of time,' laments Karel Schrijver of Lockheed Martin's Solar and Astrophysics Laboratory in California. And because the impact of a storm depends in part on how its magnetic field aligns with that of the Earth, scientists cannot be sure of the storm's intensity until it reaches the ACE satellite – sometimes a mere 20 minutes before it slams into Earth. For now, researchers concentrate on forecasting a storm's potential strength and its likely arrival time, giving vulnerable systems time to prepare. ■

Neither solid, liquid nor gas, the sun is made up of a solar plasma that's even more conductive than copper wire. Combined with the sun's magnetic fields, which power the solar wind, the plasma is driven outward at well over a million kilometres an hour by the millions of tons every second.

A coronal mass ejection from
the sun. The resulting shock-
wave can cause a disruption
in Earth's magnetic field, and
even knock out the power grid.

A pygmy marmoset feeds on sap in Yasuni National Park, Ecuador. At 10–15 centimetres long, it is the smallest primate species.

Honeymoon

Honeymoons have always been about the bride and groom getting away – it's just the reason for the getaway that has changed. In ancient Norse, the *hjunottsmanathr* was a period of time in which the groom took his bride into hiding, ensuring that after a while her family would give up searching for her and the 'happy couple' could go live

with his tribe. While in hiding, the bride and groom each would be given a daily cup of honey wine known as mead. Thirty days of mead equals 'honeymoon'.

The concept of the honeymoon as a holiday originated in 19th-century Victorian England. Industrial revolution–era advances in transportation made it easier for newlyweds to board a train or luxury steamer and explore a new locale together. ▦

Montagu's Harrier

Circus pygargus

LENGTH: 43–47 cm
WINGSPAN: 105–125 cm

This slim bird of prey soars and glides with wings held in a shallow 'V' and gives a loud, sharp display call in the form of a rapidly repeated *kniakk-kniekk-kniekk*. Its alarm call is a similar but shriller *chekk-ekk-ekk-ekk*. A summer visitor, this rare breeding bird is increasingly found nesting on arable farmland rather than in marshes. ▦

Strange . . . But True:
The Sun

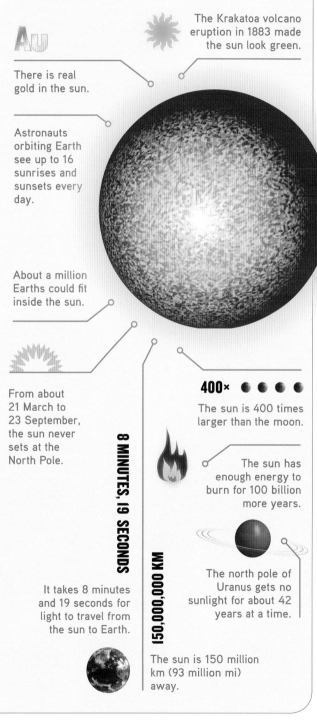

Au

There is real gold in the sun.

The Krakatoa volcano eruption in 1883 made the sun look green.

Astronauts orbiting Earth see up to 16 sunrises and sunsets every day.

About a million Earths could fit inside the sun.

From about 21 March to 23 September, the sun never sets at the North Pole.

400×

The sun is 400 times larger than the moon.

8 MINUTES, 19 SECONDS

150,000,000 KM

It takes 8 minutes and 19 seconds for light to travel from the sun to Earth.

The sun has enough energy to burn for 100 billion more years.

The north pole of Uranus gets no sunlight for about 42 years at a time.

The sun is 150 million km (93 million mi) away.

A Cinco de Mayo, or 'fifth of May,' celebration in Denver, Colorado. A day of national pride for Mexicans, it commemorates the Mexican victory at the Battle of Puebla.

SEP

THERE IS A HARMONY / IN AUTUMN AND A LUSTRE IN ITS SKY

TEMBER

Fiordland National Park, New Zealand

Webs of cascading water, veils of cloud and strands of silver beach lend mystery to New Zealand's largest national park.

Seventy per cent of New Zealanders (aka Kiwis) live on the more urban North Island. But the South Island is full of places to explore. Renting a camper van and driving around may just be the most authentic way to experience the breathtaking stretch of land that is home to Fiordland National Park, a World Heritage site.

The most accessible fjord is Milford Sound, described by Rudyard Kipling as the 'eighth wonder of the world'. Waterfalls, rain forests and stunning cliffs line the glacier-carved sound inhabited by dolphins, seals, sea lions and penguins. Spring weather typically arrives in September, though winter snow can hang on here, so plan accordingly. Queenstown, known as the 'adventure capital of the world', is a great jumping-off point for your journey – literally. It offers every adrenaline-fuelled activity you can think of: bungee jumping, paragliding, Zorbing (rolling down a hill in a giant clear plastic inflatable ball), snowboarding and more. ■

A Time-Bending Quake

An earthquake in Chile was so powerful that it is estimated to have shortened the length of a day by about 1.26 millionths of a second. The fifth strongest ever recorded, according to the U.S. Geological Survey, the magnitude 8.8 earthquake likely sped up Earth's rotation and shifted its figure axis by about eight centimetres (three inches).

The stunning scenery of Fiordland National Park, New Zealand, where the opportunities for white-knuckle sports abound

Fat-Laden Blood Gives Pythons a Boost

Python
Pythonidae
SIZE: 0.5 – 10 m
WEIGHT: 0.1 –14.5 kg
RANGE: Southern Asia, Australia, South Africa

Fat does a heart good – at least if you're a python. High levels of fatty acids, or lipids, in the reptiles' blood nearly double the size of their heart and other organs after breaking a long fast, experiments show.

The organs of pythons, which are infrequent eaters, balloon to speed up digestion after a typically enormous meal, according to study co-author Leslie Leinwand, a molecular biologist at the University of Colorado at Boulder. Until now, it's been a scientific mystery how the python's body accomplishes this 'extraordinary' feat, she says.

'When we drew blood from the animals, we figured that whatever was causing this organ growth was in the circulation, because all the organs, except the brain, had a post-meal increase in size.' Looking at the blood, Leinwand continues, 'it was so filled with fat, it was opaque – it looked like milk.'

What's most 'intriguing about the python,' says Leinwand, 'is it has this extraordinarily high level of fatty acids in its blood and [it's] not unhealthy.' By contrast, people who have fat-laden blood are often at risk for serious

The green tree python subsists on a steady diet of tree lizards, birds and small mammals.

cardiovascular conditions. Leinwand postulates that there's something about the combination of those fatty acids that thwarts disease for pythons.

Overall, it's far too early to assume the research will lead to heart-strengthening treatments for humans. But there may be heartening news to come: Leinwand's team is now giving three fatty acids to mice with heart disease to see if the lipids can prevent, slow down or even reverse their condition. ▥

STRANGE ... BUT TRUE! A python's ability to open its jaw at a 130-degree angle enables it to swallow something as large as a goat whole.

Psssstt! Superhuman Hearing Coming to an Ear Near You

People may one day be able to hear what are now inaudible sounds, scientists say.

Most people can hear sounds in the range of about 20 hertz (Hz) at the low end to about 20 kilohertz (kHz) at the high end. Twenty kHz would sound like a very high-pitched mosquito buzz and 20 Hz would be what you'd hear if you stood next to the bass at a rock concert, explains Michael Qin, a senior research scientist at the Naval Submarine Medical Research Laboratory in Connecticut.

In normal hearing, sound waves travelling through the air or water enter our ear canals and strike our eardrums, causing them to vibrate. Our eardrums are connected to three tiny bones called the malleus, incus and stapes – popularly known as the hammer, anvil and stirrup, due to their shapes.

As the stapes bone pulses back and forth, it pushes against a fluid-filled structure in the inner ear called the cochlea. Resembling a tiny snail, the cochlea contains tiny hairlike filaments that translate the pressure waves in the jostling fluid into nerve signals that are sent to the brain and interpreted as sounds.

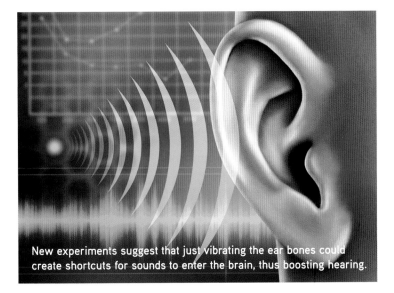

New experiments suggest that just vibrating the ear bones could create shortcuts for sounds to enter the brain, thus boosting hearing.

But very high-frequency sounds stimulate the ear bones directly, sending signals to the brain without activating the eardrums – a process known as bone-conduction hearing. This is how some species of whales hear underwater. Alternatively, certain ultrasonic frequencies might stimulate the fluid in the cochlea. 'It could be like hitting a wrench against a water tank,' Qin says. 'The fluid itself could go into oscillation.'

Qin and his team are now exploring which bones are most likely to be most sensitive to ultrasonic vibrations. Could their research lead to devices that give us superhuman hearing or improved hearing aids? Qin is silent, for now. ▪

Goldie:
Strutting Her Stuff

Goldie, a chicken living in Sydney, Australia, has an *egg-cellent* exercise routine. The big-city bird takes walks wearing a lead. 'She loves to explore the street,' says owner John Huntington, whose company City Chicks teaches city dwellers to care for hens in their back gardens.

Raising urban chickens like Goldie has become the latest trend in some cities. One reason is because people like the birds' fresh eggs. 'But chickens also make great companions,' says Ingrid Dimock, also of City Chicks. Some owners become so attached to their feathered friends that they treat the hens the same as dogs – including taking them on daily strolls.

Before Goldie goes on walks, her owner places her in a comfy harness, which attaches to her lead. Unbothered by car noises, the bird moves at a leisurely pace. And she spends as much time pecking around for grub as she does walking. 'She's kind of a slowpoke,' Huntington admits. 'But she has a lot of fun.' ▦

John Huntington takes his prized 'city chick' out for a stroll in the bustling streets of Sydney, Australia.

How To: Make a Log Float

Navigating on water can be simple or complicated, but it's imperative to have a strategy and an exit plan.

1 Cut or find two logs (the drier, the better, to increase buoyancy) at least 15 to 20 centimetres (6–8 inches) thick and about a metre or so (3–4 feet) long. Trim branches from the logs.

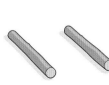

2 Tie the logs together with two ropes so that the logs lie parallel to each other about half a metre (2 feet) apart.

3 Wade into the water until it comes up over your knees. Place the logs in the water and sit between them, with your knees over the front log and your back resting against the rear log.

EXPERT TIP: If you must ride out rapids before swimming to safety or catching a rescue line, go downstream feet first, with your legs acting as shock absorbers to fend off rocks. Use a backstroke to manoeuvre past obstacles.

Impeccable table manners: four polite pooches wait to start their dinner in Narragansett Bay, Rhode Island.

Spilling Their Guts: Sicilian Mummies Bring Centuries to Life

Arrayed in crypts and churches, with leering skulls and parchment skin, the desiccated dead of Sicily have long kept mute vigil. Now, centuries later, these creepy cadavers have plenty to say.

Five years into the Sicily Mummy Project, six macabre collections are offering scientists a fresh look at life and death on the Mediterranean island from the late 16th to mid-20th centuries. Led by anthropologist Dario Piombino-Mascali of the Department of Cultural Heritage and Sicilian Identity in Palermo, the ongoing investigation is revealing how religious men and their wealthy supporters ate, interacted, dealt with disease and disposed of their dead.

In the case of the Sicilian mummies, X-ray exams and CT scans offer unique insights in biology and history. Radiographic techniques preserve the specimens, the oldest of which dates to 1599, when Capuchin friars began mummifying first clergy, then nobles and bourgeoisie who hoped to secure blessed afterlives – even as they peek inside.

What lies within? For one thing, evidence of a good diet, says Piombino-Mascali. Since most of the mummies were well-off in life, they ate a balanced mix of meat, fish, grains, vegetables and dairy products. But that gastronomic affluence came with a price. Isotopic probes of the bones also show signs of maladies like gout and skeletal disease, which Piombino-Mascali says 'tended to afflict the middle and upper classes in preindustrial societies.'

As work continues apace in Sicily, discoveries are coming from unlikely places. Karl Reinhard, a forensic scientist at the University of Nebraska–Lincoln, recently launched a pilot programme to see what he and his students could glean just by examining intestines.

Radiology revealed that one of their subjects had multiple myeloma, a form of cancer. But the real surprise came when Reinhard's student Melissa Lien found evidence of milkwort, a pollen plant with antitumor agents.

'That indicates that people here had an esoteric knowledge of medicinal plants,' says Reinhard, whose team also found traces of grape pulp, a purgative with compounds effective in cancer treatment and cardiovascular disease. 'This shows how we can create a thumbnail sketch – his disease, his diet, his time of death – from the inside of a mummy,' he says. ▪

Proper Corpse Care Mummification in Sicily usually meant draining a body of its fluids and stuffing it with straw to preserve its shape.

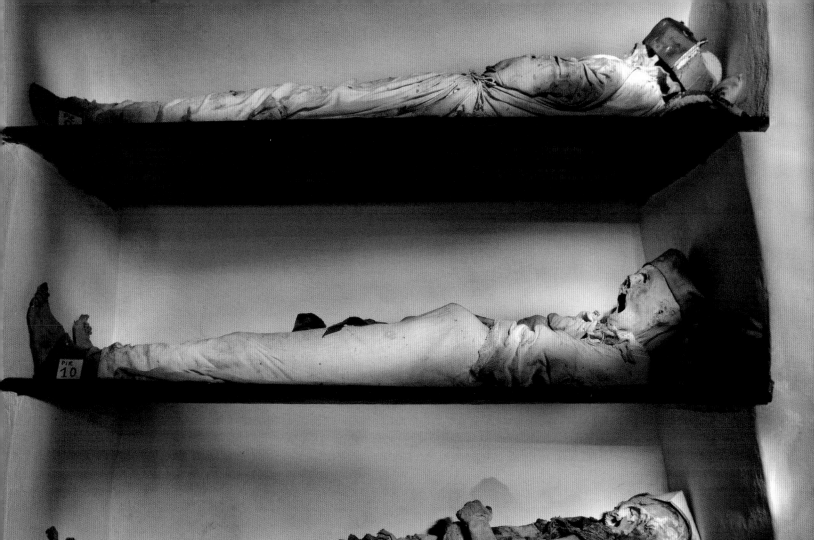

Mummies line the shelves of a crypt in Piraino, Sicily.

Double vision: a portrait taken in Twinsburg, Ohio, the site of the annual Twin Days Festival

Top Hat

The top hat is scarcely worn anymore, but it still stands for a kind of refinement and elegance that people revere. Therefore, it's ironic that on its first appearance in London streets in 1797, women supposedly fainted and children screamed to see a man sporting such a tall, shiny chapeau. It took about 20 years for top hats to truly catch on as the preferred headgear of gentlemen – after royal consort Prince Albert began to wear one.

The 19th century is sometimes called the 'century of the top hat,' although real top hats quickly fell from manufacturing favour as more easily produced bowlers and fedoras became fashionable. Since sewing top hats requires time and skill, the iconic head cover has remained a symbol of glamour, refined manners and attention to detail. ▦

Ruff

Philomachus pugnax
LENGTH: 26–32 cm
WINGSPAN: 54–58 cm

A reeve is the female counterpart of this highly sociable sandpiper, which erects its brightly coloured head and neck feathers as part of its elaborate courting display. Often travelling as part of a large flock, the ruff is rather silent, though a low single or double *kik* is sometimes given in flight. Damp meadows, bogs and freshwater marshes are common breeding grounds. ▦

Strange . . . But True:
The Ocean

Scientists know more about the surface of the moon than the bottom of the ocean.

Our planet has the same amount of water today as it did 100 million years ago.

More than 70% of the Earth's surface is water.

Half of the world's oxygen is made in the ocean.

4,267 M = OCEANS' AVERAGE DEPTH

It would take a stack of more than 9 Empire State Buildings to equal the average depth of the ocean.

NaCl × 7

The Dead Sea is 7 times saltier than the ocean.

In the open ocean, a tsunami sometimes travels as fast as a jet plane.

97% of Earth's water is saltwater.

+ + + + + < PACIFIC

More water is in the Pacific Ocean than in all of the other seas and oceans combined.

Cold water weighs more than hot water.

Gathering storm clouds don't
deter this daring motocross rider
as he hurls into a dark heaven at
Wild Rat Motocross in Colorado
Springs, Colorado.

O HUSHED OCTOBER MORNING MILD, / BEGIN THE HOURS OF THIS DAY SLOW

OCTOBER

Stuttgart, Germany

Fun – and beer – are always in high order when autumn rolls around in Deutschland, and Stuttgart offers the real deal on both fronts.

Inside a wooden tent at Stuttgart's Cannstatter Volksfest – Oktoberfest's littler, but more authentic brother

Munich's Oktoberfest may be bigger, but Stuttgart's Cannstatter Volksfest – billed as the world's second largest beer-drinking event – is considered Germany's more authentic celebration of local heritage and, of course, beer. Launched as an agricultural fair in 1818 – a symbolic 24-metre-high (78-foot) 'fruit column' pays homage to the past – the three-week festival features live music, a re-created Alpine village and carnival rides. From late September to mid-October, the action centres on massive festival tents accommodating up to 5,000 revellers each.

Between steins of pilsner, sample some traditional *Käsespätzle* (Swabian noodles with cheese) and make time to retreat to the Stuttgart region's terraced hillsides and natural mineral springs, as well as the nearby Black Forest. Recognised as a global car capital – both the Mercedes-Benz and Porsche museums are worth a visit – Stuttgart also is part of one of Germany's largest wine-growing regions. Sample this year's vintage and homemade Swabian dishes at a cosy *Besenwirtschaften* or '*Besa*' (wine inn). ▐

O₂ Overdose

Predatory dragonflies the size of modern seagulls ruled the air 300 million years ago, when the rise of vast lowland swamp forests led to atmospheric oxygen levels of around 30 per cent – close to 50 per cent higher than current levels. A new study suggests that the prehistoric creatures' body mass increased to offset the risk of oxygen poisoning.

IQs Soar When It Comes to Know-It-All Crows

Crow
Corvus
SIZE: 0.2 – 0.7 m
WEIGHT: 0.04 – 1.7 kg
RANGE: All continents except Antarctica

Clever crows are one of nature's brainiest birds, sharing the similar hallmarks of higher intelligence with humans.

Crows and humans may sit on distinct branches of the genetic tree, but there's more in common than meets the eye. Candace Savage, a nature writer based in Saskatoon, Canada, explores the burgeoning field of crow research, which suggests that the birds share with humans several hallmarks of higher intelligence, including tool use and sophisticated social behaviour.

As a sign of crows' advanced smarts, Savage cites a 2002 study by zoologist Alex Kacelnik of Oxford University. Published in *Science*, the research focuses on a captive New Caledonian crow that bent a straight piece of wire into a hook to fetch a bucket of food in a tube. 'No other animal – not even a chimp – has ever spontaneously solved a problem like this, a fact that puts crows in a class with us as toolmakers,' Savage writes in her book, *Crows: Encounters with the Wise Guys of the Avian World.*

The intelligence of other crow species, most notably ravens, is also demonstrated by their ability to manipulate the outcomes of their social interactions, according to Savage. For example, she highlights raven research by University of Vermont zoologist Bernd Heinrich showing how juvenile and adult ravens differ when feeding on a carcass. The juveniles cause a ruckus when feeding to recruit other young ravens to the scene for added safety against larger competition. The adults, by contrast, show up at a carcass in pairs and keep quiet to avoid drawing attention to – and competition for – the food. ▮

Not such a featherbrain: a study suggests that crows could have problem-solving abilities more advanced than those of chimps.

STRANGE ... BUT TRUE! Crows are very social and live in family groups consisting of between 2 and 15 birds, with 4 being the average.

Night Owls and Early Birds

Not sure if you're a morning person or a night owl? Don't worry. Your hair knows.

The genes that regulate our body clocks can be found in hair-follicle cells, researchers have discovered. A tiny portion of the brain called the suprachiasmatic nucleus controls the human body clock and RNA strands – protein-building chains of molecules – process these signals throughout the body in 24-hour cycles.

The easiest RNA for scientists to test are those in human hair. Makoto Akashi of the Research Institute for Time Studies at Yamaguchi University in Japan and his colleagues pulled head and beard hairs from four test subjects at three-hour intervals for a full day. The subjects had already reported their preferred schedules for waking up and eating, among other lifestyle choices. The test day occurred after the subjects had rigorously adhered to their preferred schedules for nine days – in other words, the morning people woke up early every day and the late sleepers woke up late every day.

When the researchers tested the genes in the subjects' follicles, they found that body-clock gene activity peaked right after a subject had woken up, regardless of whether it was 6 a.m. or 10 a.m. This suggests that the brain 'turns on' the genes at different times of the morning in different people. Other clock genes followed similar patterns, making it possible to predict 'morning people' with just a pluck, the study said.

The follicle test could be used to develop 'working conditions that do not disturb clock function' by building in enough time to adjust, the authors wrote. A noninvasive check for a clock disorder could serve as an early warning system, too. ▮

Fully Covered
Hair grows almost everywhere on your skin except your lips, the palms of your hands and the soles of your feet.

Willow:
For the Love of Learning

Once your dog has conquered riding a horse, skateboarding and learning 250 visual and verbal commands, why not teach her how to read? 'It was either that or learning how to make a martini,' jokes Lyssa Howells, who was looking to teach Willow, a terrier mix, some new tricks.

Spurred on by a bet with a friend, Howells wrote three commands on separate pieces of paper – 'Sit Up,' 'Wave' and 'Bang' (the cue to roll over on her back as if she's been shot) – and with the aid of food rewards, she taught Willow to do what was visually asked of her in a matter of weeks. 'It's repetition, just like anything,' says Howells, who is a dog trainer. 'She learned to understand that particular order of letters. What she's recognising is the meaning of a pattern of pictures, which is really what reading is.' Now the trouble is teaching her 'how *not* to listen to me,' Howells laughs. ▦

When Willow mastered all the usual tricks, her owner expanded her education to include reading.

How To: Build an A-Frame Fire

From maintaining body temperature to sending smoke signals, fire is central to survival.

1. Make an 'A' out of three pieces of wood.

2. Lean kindling perpendicular against the crossbar of the 'A' with an air space underneath it.

3. Pile dry tinder on top of the kindling.

4. Light the tinder from the bottom, through the kindling. After it catches, slowly add kindling.

5. Gradually add wood at regular intervals, leaving space for air.

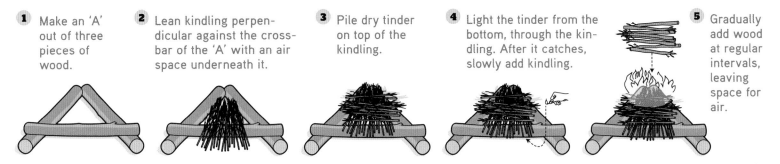

EXPERT TIP: Hardwoods such as oak, ash and birch produce a long-burning fire with lasting coals. Softwoods such as pine, spruce and cedar produce a quick, hot fire and provide excellent fuel for starting a long-burning fire with harder wood.

Mexican free-tailed bats spiral out
of Eckert James River Bat Cave
Preserve in Texas at dusk. In some
places, free-tailed bat colonies
number up to 20,000,000.

The Crop Circle Controversy

Are crop circles – flattened, gigantic patterns in farmers' fields – agrarian graffiti, large-scale land art or something more profound … an otherworldly message from outer space? No matter what side you're on, the debate fascinates and draws tens of thousands of people to the English countryside every year to have a look for themselves.

Crop circles began to appear in the fields of southern England in the mid-1970s. Early circles were quite simple and appeared overnight in fields of wheat, oilseed rape, oat and barley. The crops had been flattened, the stalks bent but not broken.

The county of Wiltshire is the acknowledged centre of the phenomenon. It is home to some of the most sacred Neolithic sites in Europe, built as far back as 4,600 years ago, including Stonehenge, Avebury, Silbury Hill and burial grounds such as West Kennet Long Barrow. As the crop circle phenomenon gained momentum, formations were also reported in Australia, South Africa, China, Russia and many other countries, frequently in close proximity to ancient sacred sites. Still, each year more than a hundred formations appeared in the fields of southern England.

During the last 25 years, the formations have evolved from simple, relatively small circles to huge designs with multiple circles, elaborate pictograms and shapes that invoke complex nonlinear mathematical principles. A formation that appeared in August 2001 at Milk Hill in Wiltshire contained 409 circles, covered about 5 hectares (12 acres) and was more than 243 metres (800 feet) across.

John Lundberg, a graphic designer, artist and website creator, has acknowledged that he made some of the circles. To combat the theory that the circles were the result of wind vortices – essentially mini-whirlwinds – Lundberg says he felt compelled to produce ever more elaborate designs, some with straight lines to show that the circles were not a natural phenomenon.

But there are researchers of the paranormal and scientists who seek to explain the formations as work that could not possibly all be the result of human efforts. Some believers are merely curious, open to the existence of paranormal activity and willing to consider the possibility that at least some of the circles were created by extraterrestrial forces.

Whatever the cause, crop circles have spawned bus tours, daily helicopter flights and sales of T-shirts, books and other trinkets. One thing's for sure, the phenomenon shows no signs of abating. ■

Loyal Following
Crop circle enthusiasts, or 'croppies', also call themselves cereologists – after Ceres, the Roman goddess of agriculture.

Crop circles were first reported in southern England in the 1970s, but have since spread to Australia, South Africa and Slovenia, where these circles were found.

Children dressed as an elephant and a bat pose at the Dodo masquerade in Burkina Faso, an event during which revellers sing and dance beneath a full moon.

Coffee

Coffee's history is as stimulating as the beverage itself. Legend has it that an Ethiopian goatherd named Kaldi discovered the plant when his goats became friskier after eating its berries. More likely is the historical fact that Ethiopian hunters and warriors learned to make primitive energy bars out of coffee cherries and animal fat rolled together.

It was the Arabs in Africa who first tried coffee as a hot beverage. *Kahve kanes,* or coffee houses, became popular in the Yemeni port of Mocha in the 11th century. Seen as an almost mystical substance, the lucrative drink was not permitted to be exported. It was eventually smuggled out by an Indian Muslim on a pilgrimage to Mecca. Once coffee arrived in Constantinople in 1475, it quickly spread to other lands.

Common Crane

Grus grus

LENGTH: 110–120 cm
WINGSPAN: 220–245 cm

The only widespread crane of the region, this powerful bird gives a loud, far-carrying *krooh* or a harsher *krah*. Adults often duet on breeding grounds, giving a more musical *krooh-krii … krooh-kri.* Outside the season for breeding, which typically takes place in bogs and swampy forest clearings, cranes are found in large flocks in open country.

Strange … But True:
Population

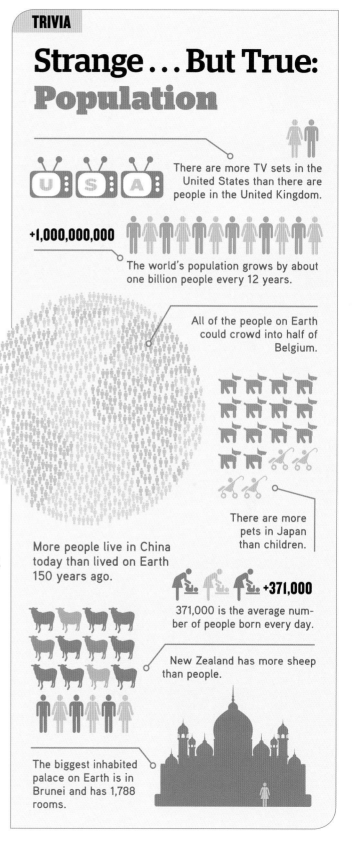

There are more TV sets in the United States than there are people in the United Kingdom.

+1,000,000,000

The world's population grows by about one billion people every 12 years.

All of the people on Earth could crowd into half of Belgium.

There are more pets in Japan than children.

More people live in China today than lived on Earth 150 years ago.

+371,000

371,000 is the average number of people born every day.

New Zealand has more sheep than people.

The biggest inhabited palace on Earth is in Brunei and has 1,788 rooms.

Hundreds of hot-air balloons float in a powder-blue sky at the Albuquerque International Balloon Fiesta in New Mexico, a tradition that spans more than four decades.

NO

THE THINNEST YELLOW LIGHT OF NOVEMBER IS MORE WARMING AND EXHILARATING THAN ANY WINE

VEMBER

The Himalaya, India

Pure air, exhilarating views and fascinating flora in the western Himalaya will bring you closer to the essence of life than most vacations.

Starkly beautiful: a creek cuts through the dry land below the remote peak of Garhwal Himalaya, in the Indian state of Uttarakhand.

The Himalaya, the world's highest mountains, are less than 130 million years old and still growing. When the ancient geological plate of the Indian peninsula – some three billion years old – moved under the Asian plate, the dramatic crumpling and fissuring began. The Himalaya began to rise and they continue to do so today.

As a contrast to the heady cocktail of monuments, history, heat and city crowds in India, a hike in the foothills of the Himalaya will invigorate you. October and November offer the clearest views of the high peaks. The cool air, mountain scenery, culture and lifestyle promise relaxation after touring the plains, and the lower slopes in Uttarakhand or Himachal Pradesh are easily accessible from Delhi.

The more ambitious can press on to Ladakh – an isolated and starkly beautiful spot that is one of the large refuges of Mahayana Buddhism. Medieval monasteries, perched on craggy cliffs and known locally as *gompas,* are still centres of learning and worship, housing remarkable artefacts like wall paintings and unusual musical instruments. ∎

Not Just Monkeying Around

In India, monkey business takes on a whole new meaning. Hanuman langurs are trained in New Delhi to scare off aggressive rhesus monkeys and other wild animals that might roam into public spaces. Named for a Hindu god, these primates are not only valued security guards but also revered to holy status in some cities.

Oddities Dropped From Orbit

To date, nearly 6,000 tons of human-made material has survived the fiery journey through our atmosphere, according to the Aerospace Corporation of California. Here are some of the notable objects that have made surprise return trips to Earth:

1: Sphere of Influence

In 2011, a hiker in north-western Colorado spotted a spherical object, still warm to the touch, sitting in a crater. A tank from a Russian Zenit-3 rocket, it is one of the few such space objects to be recovered in the United States.

2: Brush With Space Junk

A woman taking a late-night walk in Oklahoma in January 1997 saw a streak of light in the sky, then felt something brush her shoulder. It turned out to be part of a U.S. Delta II rocket launched in 1996 – the only space debris ever known to have hit someone, according to the Aerospace Corporation. The woman was unhurt – and lucky. NASA reports that a 260-kilogram (580-pound) fuel tank from the same rocket slammed to the ground in Texas around the same time, narrowly missing an occupied farmhouse.

3: Nuclear Waste

In January 1978, the Soviet surveillance satellite Kosmos 954 crashed in northern

In the case of space junk, what goes up sometimes comes back down – a bizarre range of man-made objects have plummeted from orbit back to Earth.

Canada, scattering radioactive material from the spacecraft's nuclear power generator over thousands of square kilometres. The Canadian government mounted a frantic campaign dubbed Operation Morning Light to find the radioactive material, but only 0.1 per cent of the dangerous debris was ever recovered.

4: Space Station Shower

When the Salyut 7 space station began trailing lower in its orbit, Soviet engineers tried to send it into a controlled tumble into the Atlantic Ocean. But their efforts failed and the massive station – one of the largest human-made objects to reenter the atmosphere – showered metal fragments on a city in Argentina, where residents observed glowing trails in the sky. No one was hurt, according to the U.S. Aerospace Corporation. ▧

STRANGE … BUT TRUE! There's a one in a trillion chance that a piece of space junk will land on your house today.

Battle of the Sexes

It's well known that men and women don't always see eye to eye. But now we're closer to understanding the gender-based differences at play.

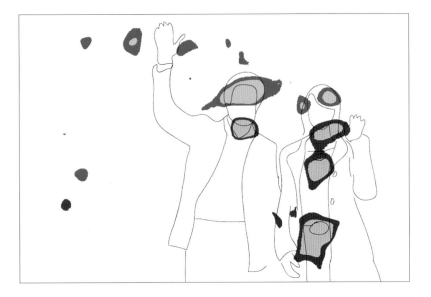

A new study shows that men and women literally focus on different things. The diagram shows the most eye-catching areas of the photo above for men (blue) and women (red).

A new study published in *PLoS One* finds that males and females actually view images in different ways. When University of Bristol researchers in the United Kingdom asked 52 men and women to study various images, gender differences emerged in terms of where the subjects focused their attention and how much of a picture they explored.

The 26 female and 26 male study participants, ranging in age from 19 to 47, were shown still images from films and of artwork. The images included scenes from movies such as *The Sound of Music, Inside Man* and *The Blue Planet* and artwork including 'People in the Sun' by Edward Hopper and 'Three Graces' by David Bowers.

The participants tended to focus on anywhere from one to five 'hot spots' in the pictures. Most of the hot spots involved the faces of people in the pictures, especially their eyes, as well as other body parts such as hands. Women, however, explored more of an image than men did, often focusing on nonfacial areas and places slightly below where men fixed their gaze.

Lead author Felix Mercer Moss, a vision researcher and doctoral student at the university, speculates that risk aversion may explain some of the differences. In Western culture, a direct gaze can be construed as threatening.

Research on gender differences in eye movements isn't new, Mercer Moss says, but previous studies used specific imagery, such as faces registering emotions or sexually suggestive pictures. In this study, he wanted to know whether gender differences existed when people viewed more general visual stimuli. It turns out they do – suggesting that beauty isn't the only thing in the eye of the beholder. ▪

Charlie:

Will Wave for Food

Charlie the harbour seal knows how to get people's attention: he waves at them. The marine mammal isn't greeting visitors with a hearty hello, though; he's hoping for some food.

Whenever tourists arrive at his harbour in Dublin, Ireland, with bits of fish to feed the seals, Charlie starts motioning. He sticks his flipper out of the water and flaps it back and forth until the visitors throw him a snack. 'Out of all the seals, Charlie definitely gets the most food – and the most laughs,' says wildlife photographer Paul Hughes, who has snapped pictures of the hungry seal's gestures.

Ordinarily, seals will wave when they're overheated or trying to warn away other seals. 'But these animals are very smart,' says Sheryl Fink, a director at the International Fund for Animal Welfare. 'Charlie seems to have learned that he'll be rewarded with food if he waves.' This savvy seal deserves a hand. ■

Charlie the seal knows how to work the tourist trade in Dublin. He's learnt that a quick wave could earn him some dinner.

How To: Build an Apache Shelter

For an unplanned overnight stay, use brush to build a basic ventilated shelter.

1 Gather five or six ten-foot branches and arrange in a circle with tops leaning together at a 45-degree angle.

2 Add more support poles, leaning them together in the same manner.

3 Brace with flexible, horizontal willow branches or weave cord or rope around the circumference to create latticework.

4 Gather the thatching—any dried leaves you can find —and attach from the bottom up.

EXPERT TIP: A tarp is the simplest form of outdoor shelter; it weighs very little and can be set up in dozens of ways. Use it as your primary shelter or to protect your group's gear.

Awestruck tourists gaze at Niagara's famous Horseshoe Falls. Their yellow macs repel the spray from the enormous volume of water crashing down.

Earthquakes: A Waiting Game

Generations of scientists and folklorists have used a dizzying array of methods to attempt to predict earthquakes. Animal behaviour, changes in the weather and seismograms have all fallen short. Could magnetic waves be the trustworthy tool that saves lives?

The dream is to be able to forecast earthquakes like we now predict the weather. Even a few minutes' warning would be enough for people to move away from walls or ceilings that might collapse or for nuclear plants and other critical facilities to be shut down safely in advance of a quake. And if accurate predictions could be made a few days in advance, any necessary evacuations could be planned, much as is done today for hurricanes.

One theory is that when an earthquake looms, the rock 'goes through a strange change' that produces intense electrical currents, says Tom Bleier, a satellite engineer with QuakeFinder, a project funded by his parent company, Stellar Solutions of Cambridge, Massachusetts. 'These currents are huge,' Bleier reported at a meeting of the American Geophysical Union. 'They're on the order of 100,000 amperes for a magnitude 6 earthquake and a million amperes for a magnitude 7. It's almost like lightning, underground.'

To measure those currents, Bleier's team has spent millions of dollars putting out magnetometers along fault lines in California, Peru, Taiwan and Greece. The instruments are sensitive enough to detect magnetic pulses from electrical discharges up to 16 kilometres (10 miles) away. 'The fault is always moving, grinding, snapping and crackling,' he explained. Before a large earthquake, that background level of static electricity discharges should rise sharply.

And that is indeed what Bleier claims he's seen prior to the half dozen magnitude 5 and 6 earthquakes whose precursors he's been able to monitor. 'It goes up to maybe 150 or 200 pulses a day.' The number of pulses, he added, seems to surge about two weeks before the earthquake, then to return to background level until shortly before the fault slips.

But magnetic pulses could be caused by a lot of other things, ranging from random events within the Earth to lightning, solar flares and electrical interference from highway equipment. Bleier's team hasn't yet monitored enough quakes for him to be sure that what he's found is valid, but he does feel they have enough good clues to move ahead. ∎

Animal Instinct
Around 2,300 years ago, hordes of mice, snakes and insects fled the Greek city of Helike. 'After these creatures departed, an earthquake occurred in the night,' recorded the ancient Roman writer Claudius Aelianus. 'The city subsided; an immense wave flooded and Helike disappeared.'

San Francisco is one of the earthquake-prone cities that would benefit from technology that monitors magnetic pulses to predict seismic events.

Stand back: an Indochinese tigress shakes herself dry after a swim at Khao Kheow Open Zoo in Chon-buri, Thailand.

Buttons

Buttons and buttonholes seem like a natural combination, but it took returning crusaders to bring the concept back to the West from the 'barbarian' Turks and Mongols. The first buttons seem to have functioned more as a decorative element than an actual fastener.

It will surprise no one that the first Button Makers Guild was formed in clothing-conscious France, in 1250. Members of the guild produced buttons so exquisite that they were truly tiny pieces of jewellery, while the peasantry was forbidden to use buttons made of anything but plain cloth or thread.

As a practical closure, buttons changed not only the decoration of clothing but the entire shape. Clothes could now be made to emphasise the human form, leading to specialisation and greater demand for the tailor's profession. ▨

Eurasian Oystercatcher

Haematopus ostralegus

LENGTH: 40–46 cm
WINGSPAN: 80–86 cm

A high, shrill, piping *kleep* is the voice of this distinctive wader. Breeding birds accelerate the piping trill into a Eurasian curlew–like trill before trailing away: *ke-beep, ke-beep, ke-beep, kwirrrrrrr, ee-beep, ee-beep, ee-beep.* The species is commonly found in a wide variety of rocky, sandy or muddy coastal habitats. ▨

Strange . . . But True:
Sleep

JUST A NAP

Some snails can sleep for 3 years.

☀ **x 10**
The longest anyone has gone without sleep is 10 days.

Koalas stay awake for only 4 hours a day.

A 15-year-old cat has probably spent 10 years of its life sleeping.

Newborn dolphins sleep for only a few seconds at a time.

Babies yawn before they are born.

+ 1,500
Adults have as many as 1,500 dreams a year.

You can't move your body when you're dreaming.

It takes the average 10-year-old child about 20 minutes to fall asleep.

Riders on the chairoplanes at Hyde Park's Winter Wonderland fair in London enjoy the thrill of the fresh air on a crisp afternoon.

DE

LATE LIES THE WINTRY SUN A-BED, / A FROSTY, FIERY SLEEPY-HEAD

CEMBER

New York City, United States

Celebrate the season among the bright lights of the big city, where the wintry frenzy is unparallelled.

Beginning in late November, the holiday spirit in New York becomes contagious. From 34th Street to Rockefeller Center and along Madison Avenue, the air buzzes with excitement and the streets are laced with glowing lights and the aroma of roasted chestnuts.

Put on your parka and browse the gallery of window displays. Created by set designers and artists, these mini winterscapes and nostalgic interiors unfold before your eyes, along with whimsical holiday characters and remakes of Christmas movie scenes. Shoppers scouting for the perfect gift gravitate toward the Holiday Market at Union Square, where festive striped tents are brimming with souvenirs like handmade jewellery and old-fashioned toys.

Of course, no holiday trip is complete without a visit to the towering Christmas tree that graces Rockefeller Center. The spruce, which averages about 24 metres (80 feet) high, is dressed with more than 8 kilometres (5 miles) of lights and a Swarovski crystal star at the top. ▤

Ever-vibrant New York City pulses with energy and cheer during the run-up to Christmas, particularly around the huge tree that's the centrepiece of the Rockefeller Center.

Sleep on It

Your body may be resting during those 40 winks, but the brain is hard at work. The sleeping brain is busy 'calculating' what to remember and what to forget, a new study says. Measurements of brain activity reveal that brain regions linked with emotion and memory consolidation are periodically more active during sleep than while awake.

Salt Cravings Drive Goats to New Heights

Alpine Ibex Goat
Capra ibex
SIZE: 1.3 – 1.5 m
WEIGHT: Up to 120 kg
RANGE: European Alps

Using moves that would make any rock climber jealous, Alpine ibex scaled the near-vertical face of the 49-metre-tall (160-foot) Cingino Dam in northern Italy, as shown in pictures taken by hiker Adriano Migliorati.

The goats are attracted to the dam's salt-crusted stones, according to the U.K.-based Caters news agency. Grazing animals don't get enough of the mineral in their vegetarian diets, so these ibex scale the dam to get a fix.

Cingino Dam isn't completely vertical, allowing them to gain some purchase. Adapted to their perilous environment, Alpine ibex have evolved a specialised split hoof, whose cleft is wider than on any other split-hooved species, according to *Smithsonian* magazine. The hoof also has a hard wall that can grab on to steep cliffs and a soft, rubbery inside that serves as a 'stopper' when the animal is pushed forward by gravity, the magazine reported.

Because dams are usually built in steep canyons, Cingino's steep rock face is likely nothing novel for the mountain-dwelling ibex, according to Jeff Opperman, senior adviser for sustainable hydropower at the U.S.-based not-for-

Fearless goats scale the near-vertical Cingino Dam in northern Italy to satisfy their salt cravings.

profit the Nature Conservancy. The herbivores spend their lives scrambling the European Alps' rocky and steep terrain. By scaling Cingino Dam, Opperman says, salt-craving ibex are 'showing ingenuity, taking advantage of this human-created thing in their environment.'

Goats' eyes have rectangular pupils, which, when dilated, give them 320- to 340-degree vision.

Ball in Your Head

The mysterious floating blobs of light known as ball lightning might simply be hallucinations caused by overstimulated brains, research suggests.

For hundreds of years, eyewitnesses have reported brief encounters with golf- to tennis-ball-size orbs of electricity. But scientists have been unable to agree on how and why ball lightning forms, since the phenomenon is apparently rare and very short lived.

Ball lightning is said to float near the ground, sometimes bouncing off the ground or other objects and does not obey the whims of wind or the laws of gravity. The phenomenon typically glows with the power of a 100-watt bulb and lasts only a short time, perhaps ten seconds, before either fading away or violently dissipating with a small explosion.

Because ball lightning is often reported during thunderstorms and it's known that multiple consecutive lightning strikes can create strong magnetic fields, Joseph Peer and Alexander Kendl at the University of Innsbruck in Austria wondered whether ball lightning is really a hallucination induced by magnetic stimulation of the brain's visual cortex or the eye's retina.

Others argue that ball lightning is still feasible in nature and in the lab. John Abrahamson, a chemist and ball lightning expert at the University of Canterbury in New Zealand, points out

A 19th-century illustration depicts the mysterious phenomenon known as ball lightning, in which a floating fireball comes suddenly into view. Is it a figment of the imagination caused by electromagnetic stimulation, or a very real anomaly?

that some eyewitness reports of ball lightning include close-up observations detailing the internal structures of the balls and even associated smells and sounds. Some instances even involve multiple eyewitnesses who saw the same phenomenon from different angles and saw the balls travel in the same directions. 'This common geometric perception from different angles would be very unlikely if their brains were being stimulated' by the local magnetic field caused by lightning strikes, according to Abrahamson.

Jasmine:
The Friendliest Dog in Town

No one ever expected Jasmine to love again. In 2003, English police discovered a greyhound cowering in a locked shed, malnourished and clearly abused. They brought her to the Nuneaton & Warwickshire Wildlife Sanctuary, founded and run by Geoff Grewcock with the intent of caring for sick and injured animals.

Determined to nurse her back to health, Grewcock and his staff showered Jasmine with affection. 'Within a month, she became a loving dog,' he recalls. Jasmine's nurturing instinct first showed itself with a pair of abandoned puppies. When they arrived, Jasmine approached as a mother dog would: licking them and picking them up in her mouth to carry them around the property. There are certain things only an animal mother can provide and Jasmine provided it, says Grewcock.

But Jasmine didn't stop with the puppies. Bramble, an 11-week-old orphaned fawn, received the same attention – as did 5 fox cubs, 4 badger cubs, 15 chicks, 8 guinea pigs and 15 rabbits. Jasmine's love knew no boundaries; the rescued was soon doing the rescuing. ▤

Jasmine, a rescued greyhound, cared for more than 50 animals, including an orphaned fawn named Bramble.

How To: Signal With an Improvised Mirror
In lieu of a mobile connection, a polished surface can enable communication.

1 Hold a piece of glass, polished metal or aluminium foil in one hand. Place your other hand at arm's length in front of it and make a 'V' with the fingers of that hand. Wiggle the improvised mirror until reflected sunlight passes through your fingers, then sight along your arm.

2 If the angle between the sun and the rescue aircraft is less than 90 degrees, the mirror will nearly face the plane.

3 If the angle between the sun and the rescue plane is between 90 and 180 degrees, hold the mirror at a shallower angle.

4 In either case, aim the mirror at a point halfway between the sun and the intended target of reflected light.

EXPERT TIP: Light signals work best when operated from open, high terrain, such as the top of a mountain ridge. Such sites are also good for lighting signal fires at night and smoke signals during the day.

VISIONS OF EARTH

A stunning rainbow arcs across the horizon as a fisherman and a young girl move through the placid waters of the Philippines' Palawan Islands.

Cave of Wonders: Mexico's Giant Crystals

A team of geologists has solved the mystery behind the formation of giant crystals in a Mexican cave known as the 'Sistine Chapel of crystals'.

Buried 300 metres (1,000 feet) below Naica Mountain in the Chihuahuan Desert, this spectacular wonder was discovered by two miners excavating a new tunnel for the Industrias Peñoles company in 2000. They found a cave filled with some of the largest known natural crystals: translucent gypsum beams measuring up to 11 metres (36 feet) long and weighing up to 55 tons.

To learn how the crystals grew to such gigantic sizes, Juan Manuel García-Ruiz of the University of Granada in Spain studied tiny pockets of fluid trapped inside. The crystals, he determined, thrived because they were submerged in mineral-rich water with a very narrow, stable temperature range – around 58°C (136°F). At this temperature, the mineral anhydrite, which was abundant in the water, dissolved into gypsum, a soft mineral that can take the form of the crystals in the Naica cave.

The Cave of Crystals is a horseshoe-shaped cavity in limestone rock about 9.1 metres (30 feet) wide and 27.4 metres (90 feet) long. Its floor is covered in crystalline, perfectly faceted blocks. The huge crystal beams jut out from both the blocks and the floor.

Volcanic activity that began about 26 million years ago created Naica Mountain and filled it with high-temperature anhydrite, which is the anhydrous – lacking water – form of gypsum. Anhydrite is stable above 58°C (136°F). Below that temperature, gypsum is the stable form.

When magma underneath the mountain cooled and the temperature dropped below 58°C, the anhydrite began to dissolve. The anhydrite slowly enriched the waters with sulphate and calcium molecules, which for millions of years have been deposited in the caves in the form of huge selenite gypsum crystals. 'There is no limit to the size a crystal can reach,' García-Ruiz says.

But, he says, for the Cave of Crystals to have grown such gigantic crystals, it must have been kept just below the anhydrite-gypsum transition temperature for many hundreds of thousands of years. While the chance of this set of conditions occurring in other places in the world is remote, García-Ruiz expects that there are other caves and caverns at Naica containing similarly large crystals. ▨

Looters, Beware The Cave of Crystals' stifling temperatures and the fact that it takes 20 minutes to drive to its entrance through a twisting mine shaft haven't prevented looters from trying to get a piece of the treasure. One of the crystals was found with a deep scar where someone tried, but failed, to cut through it.

Massive beams of selenite crystals dwarf explorers in the Cave of Crystals deep below Mexico's Chihuahuan Desert.

Not as cuddly as they look: snow powder flies as two polar bears spar for supremacy in Wapusk National Park in Canada.

Sledding

Tobogganing most likely began with small sledges that were used to haul cargo. Algonquin hunters built *odabaggans* made of birch or hickory strips to pull their game and supplies across the snow. Later Indians crafted canoe-shaped

toboggans outfitted with wooden runners. After about 1870, the coasting, or clipper, sledge with steel rods for runners became common on the snow-covered slopes of American villages.

By the 1880s, coasting had popularised as an activity, especially in the fashionable resorts of Switzerland, where it was known as tobogganing. Runs were built and competitions evolved into the sport of skeleton, in which the racer lies prone, headfirst on a ribbed frame sledge. Skeleton was a winter Olympic event in St. Moritz in 1928 and 1948 before becoming a permanent event in 2002. ▦

Northern Gannet

Morus bassanus

LENGTH: 87–100 cm

WINGSPAN: 165–180 cm

The largest breeding seabird of the region, the northern gannet repeats a loud, throaty *urrah* at colonies and while feeding communally. The birds tend to breed on rocky islets and sea cliffs on small islands and they migrate as far south as subtropical or even tropical West Africa. ▦

Strange ... But True: Cold Weather

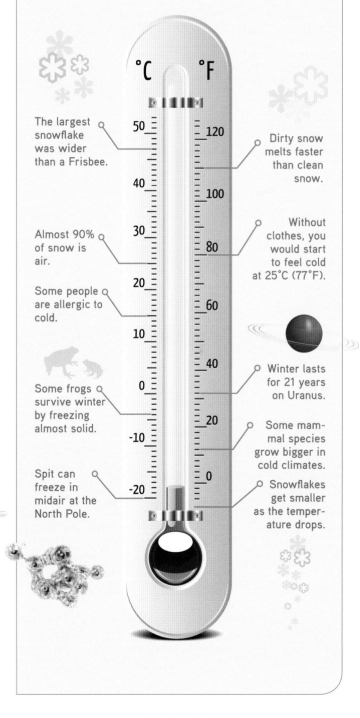

The largest snowflake was wider than a Frisbee.

Almost 90% of snow is air.

Some people are allergic to cold.

Some frogs survive winter by freezing almost solid.

Spit can freeze in midair at the North Pole.

Dirty snow melts faster than clean snow.

Without clothes, you would start to feel cold at 25°C (77°F).

Winter lasts for 21 years on Uranus.

Some mammal species grow bigger in cold climates.

Snowflakes get smaller as the temperature drops.

2014 Calendar

January

S	M	T	W	T	F	S
			1	2	3	4
5	6	7	8	9	10	11
12	13	14	15	16	17	18
19	20	21	22	23	24	25
26	27	28	29	30	31	

February

S	M	T	W	T	F	S
						1
2	3	4	5	6	7	8
9	10	11	12	13	14	15
16	17	18	19	20	21	22
23	24	25	26	27	28	

March

S	M	T	W	T	F	S
						1
2	3	4	5	6	7	8
9	10	11	12	13	14	15
16	17	18	19	20	21	22
23/30 24/31	25	26	27	28	29	

April

S	M	T	W	T	F	S
		1	2	3	4	5
6	7	8	9	10	11	12
13	14	15	16	17	18	19
20	21	22	23	24	25	26
27	28	29	30			

May

S	M	T	W	T	F	S
				1	2	3
4	5	6	7	8	9	10
11	12	13	14	15	16	17
18	19	20	21	22	23	24
25	26	27	28	29	30	31

June

S	M	T	W	T	F	S
1	2	3	4	5	6	7
8	9	10	11	12	13	14
15	16	17	18	19	20	21
22	23	24	25	26	27	28
29	30					

July

S	M	T	W	T	F	S
		1	2	3	4	5
6	7	8	9	10	11	12
13	14	15	16	17	18	19
20	21	22	23	24	25	26
27	28	29	30	31		

August

S	M	T	W	T	F	S
					1	2
3	4	5	6	7	8	9
10	11	12	13	14	15	16
17	18	19	20	21	22	23
24/31	25	26	27	28	29	30

September

S	M	T	W	T	F	S
	1	2	3	4	5	6
7	8	9	10	11	12	13
14	15	16	17	18	19	20
21	22	23	24	25	26	27
28	29	30				

October

S	M	T	W	T	F	S
			1	2	3	4
5	6	7	8	9	10	11
12	13	14	15	16	17	18
19	20	21	22	23	24	25
26	27	28	29	30	31	

November

S	M	T	W	T	F	S
						1
2	3	4	5	6	7	8
9	10	11	12	13	14	15
16	17	18	19	20	21	22
23/30	24	25	26	27	28	29

December

S	M	T	W	T	F	S
	1	2	3	4	5	6
7	8	9	10	11	12	13
14	15	16	17	18	19	20
21	22	23	24	25	26	27
28	29	30	31			

Resources

National Geographic Books

National Geographic Books is a global publisher of 125 new books annually in Adult and Children's combined, as well as a publisher of digital content and services with more than 50 partners who translate our books. For more information on National Geographic Books, visit *facebook.com/Nat-GeoBooks* and *nationalgeographic.com/books*.

***National Geographic* magazine**

National Geographic magazine has a long tradition of combining on-the-ground reporting with award-winning photography to inform people about life on our planet. It has won 12 National Magazine Awards in the past five years: for Best Tablet Edition in 2012; Magazine of the Year and Single-Topic Issue in 2011; for General Excellence, Photojournalism and Essays, plus two Digital Media Awards for Best Photography and Best Community, in 2010; for Photojournalism in 2009; and for General Excellence, Photojournalism and Reporting in 2008.

The magazine is the official journal of the National Geographic Society, one of the world's largest nonprofit education and scientific organisations. Published in English and 37 local-language editions, the magazine has a global circulation of around 8 million. It is sent each month to National Geographic members and is available on newsstands for £4.95 a copy. Single copies can be ordered by calling 3120-487-4115, also the number to call for membership to the Society.

To submit a favourite photo for possible publication in *National Geographic* magazine, visit the Your Shot page at *http://ngm. nationalgeographic.com/your-shot*.

***National Geographic Traveler* magazine**

National Geographic Traveler: All travel, all the time. *National Geographic Traveler* is the world's most widely read travel magazine. Published eight times a year, *Traveler* is available by subscription (3120-487-4115). Its website is at *www.nationalgeographic .com/traveler*.

National Geographic Digital Media

National Geographic Digital Media (NGDM) is the multimedia division of National Geographic Ventures. Holding many top industry awards, NGDM publishes Nationalgeographic.com, including its daily online news service. With a focus on developments in the fields of science, nature and cultures, National Geographic's Daily News provides access to the top stories that are changing our world. For more information, visit *http://news.nationalgeographic .com/news/*.

Text Credits

Reprinted by arrangement from the book *Tales of the Weird.* Copyright © 2012 National Geographic Society. 16, 'Instinctual Cravings'; 36, 'Think I'm a Clone Now'; 37, 'Look, Ma! They've Got Hands!'; 48, 'The Secret Language of Stripes'; 49, 'Spawn of Medieval Black "Death Bug" Still Roam the Earth'; 50, 'Vampire Forensics: Skull of the Undead'; 62, 'Without a Trace'; 72, 'Fantastic Voyage'; 74, 'How the Nose Knows'; 110, *'Psssstt!* Superhuman Hearing Coming to an Ear Near You'; 120, 'O$_2$ Overdose'; 121, 'IQs Soar When It Comes to Know-It-All Crows'; 122, 'Night Owls and Early Birds'; 126-127, 'The Crop Circle Controversy'; 144, 'Sleep on It'; 145, 'Salt Cravings Drive Goats to New Heights'; 146, 'Ball in Your Head'; 150-151, 'Cave of Wonders: Mexico's Giant Crystals'

Reprinted by arrangement from the book *An Uncommon History of Common Things* by Bethanne Patrick and John Thompson. Copyright © 2009 National Geographic Society. 21, 'Fireworks'; 33, 'Red Roses'; 45, 'St. Patrick's Day'; 57, 'Credit Cards'; 69, 'Chess'; 81, 'Bicycle'; 93, 'Ice Cream'; 105, 'Honeymoon'; 117, 'Top Hat'; 129, 'Coffee'; 141, 'Buttons'; 153, 'Sledding'

Reprinted by arrangement from the book *Complete Survival Manual* by Michael S. Sweeny. Copyright © 2009 National Geographic Society. 17, 'How To: Make Your Own Snowshoes'; 27, 'How To: Ice-Fish'; 39, 'How To: Make a Compass'; 51, 'How To: Make a Whistle Out of an Acorn Cap'; 63, 'How To: Make a Shadow Stick'; 75, 'How To: Collect Water From Dew'; 87, 'How To: Improvise Sunglasses'; 99, 'How To: Make an Anti-Rodent Bag'; 111, 'How To: Make a Log Float'; 123, 'How To: Build an A-Frame Fire'; 135, 'How To: Build an Apache Shelter'; 147, 'How To: Signal With an Improvised Mirror'

Illustrations credits

Cover, Steve Bloom Images/Alamy; Back Cover, Octavio Aburto; 2-3, Dean Conger/NGS; 4-5, Nick Selway/National Geographic Your Shot; 6, Mustafiz Mamun/National Geographic Your Shot; 8, John Booth/National Geographic Your Shot; 10-11, Kent Shiraishi/National Geographic Your Shot; 12 (LE), Doug Pearson/Getty Images; 12 (RT), Goncharuk/Shutterstock; 13 (LE), Joel Sartore/NGS; 13 (RT UP), yui/Shutterstock; 13 (RT LO), Tatiana Popova/Shutterstock; 14-15, Paul Nicklen/NGS; 16 (UP), andersphoto/Shutterstock; 16 (LO), picamaniac/Shutterstock; 17, TPG Top Photo Group/Newscom; 18, Tom Vezo/Minden Pictures/National Geographic Stock; 19, Lynn Johnson/National Geographic Stock; 20, Wild Wonders of Europe/O. Haarberg/Naturepl.com/National Geographic Stock; 21 (LE UP), Deymos/Shutterstock; 21 (LE LO), David Quinn; 21 (RT), Sebastian Kaulitzki/Shutterstock; 22-23, Andy Parant/National Geographic Your Shot; 24 (LE), Don Fuchs/Getty Images; 24 (RT), ALMA (ESO/NAOJ/NRAO))/L. Calçada (ESO); 25 (LE), David Hu and Nathan J. Mlot; 25 (RT UP), Potapov Alexander/Shutterstock; 25 (RT LO), Henrik Larsson/Shutterstock; 26 (LE UP), Björn Meyer/iStockphoto; 26 (LE LO), Nicole S. Young/iStockphoto; 26 (RT), stockshoppe/Shutterstock; 27, DPA/Landov; 28-29, Bobby Sudekum/National Geographic Your Shot; 30, Nick Woods/Woods Hole Oceanographic Institution; 31, Brian J. Skerry/NGS; 32, Shivji Joshi/National Geographic Your Shot; 33 (LE UP), Wolfgang Amri/Shutterstock; 33 (LE LO), David Quinn; 33 (RT—chewing gum), Madlen/Shutterstock; 33 (RT—chocolate), Lipskiy/Shutterstock; 33 (RT—cookie), MariusdeGraf/Shutterstock; 33 (RT—pie), Matt Antonino/Shutterstock; 33 (RT—candy cane), photastic/Shutterstock; 33 (RT—cake), Finomax/Shutterstock; 34-35, Laura Kalcheff/National Geographic Your Shot; 36 (LE), Andoni Canela/Age Fotostock/Getty Images; 36 (RT), Morphart Creation/Shutterstock; 37 (LE), Fred Bavendam/Minden Pictures/Corbis; 37 (RT), heromen30/Shutterstock; 38, Michael Ochs Archives/Getty Images; 39, AP Photo/Kerstin Joensson; 40-41, Mikey Schaefer; 42, Marques/Shutterstock; 43, Michael Nichols, NGP; 44, Rahul Talukder/National Geographic Your Shot; 45 (LE UP), ULKASTUDIO/Shutterstock; 45 (LE LO), David Quinn; 45 (RT), Neyro/Shutterstock; 46-47, Joni Romnes Welzien/National Geographic Your Shot; 48 (LE), Mircea BEZERGHEANU/Shutterstock; 48 (RT), Ultrashock/Shutterstock; 49 (UP), "The Black Death," 1348 (engraving) (b&w photo), English School, (14th century)/Private Collection/The Bridgeman Art Library; 49 (LO), Eye of Science/Science Source; 50, AP Photo/Matteo Borrini of Florence University, HO; 51, Julia Hahn-Gallego, sceno; 52-53, Nancie Battaglia/*Sports Illustrated*/Getty Images; 54, suns07/Shutterstock; 55, Michael Nichols, NGP; 56, Martin Oeggerli/NGS; 57 (LE UP), Alexei Daniline/Shutterstock; 57 (LE LO), David Quinn; 57 (RT—hourglass), Sashkin/Shutterstock; 57 (RT—planets), Both planets: Torian/Shutterstock; 58-59, Emir Ibrahimpasic/National Geographic Your Shot; 60 (LE), Philip Lange/Shutterstock; 60 (RT), Herman in den Bosch/ Foto Natura/Minden Pictures/Getty Images; 61 (UP), MANSILIYA YURY/Shutterstock; 61 (CTR), Joel Sartore/National Geographic Stock; 61 (LO), imagebroker/Alamy; 62 (LE), David Alary/Shutterstock; 62 (RT), Jaros/Shutterstock; 63, Tibor Jager; 64-65, Aung Pyae Soe/National Geographic Your Shot; 66, David Coventry/NGS; 67, David Coventry/NGS; 68, Diane Cook & Len Jenshel; 69 (LE UP), pio3/Shutterstock; 69 (LE LO), David Quinn; 69 (RT), Maxx-Studio/Shutterstock; 70-71, Ben Hicks/National Geographic Your Shot; 72 (LE), Raymond Choo/National Geographic Your Shot; 72 (RT), Photograph courtesy Shinichiro Wada; 73 (LE), Karoline Cullen/iStockphoto; 73 (RT), Gemenacom/Shutterstock; 74, Khamidulin Sergey/Shutterstock; 75, Splash News/Newscom; 76-77, Andy Yu/National Geographic Your Shot; 78-79, Hugh Turvey/NGS; 80, Mark Leong/NGS; 81 (LE UP), Saveliev Alexey Alexsandrovich/Shutterstock; 81 (LE LO), David Quinn; 81 (RT), Sebastian Kaulitzki/Shutterstock; 82-

83, Mark Tipple/National Geographic Your Shot; 84 (LE), Aleksandar Vrzalski/iStockphoto; 84 (RT), Rikke Louise Meyer; 85 (LE), John Kimbler/National Geographic Your Shot; 85 (RT UP), BS_Lexx/Shutterstock; 85 (RT LO), Butterfly Hunter/Shutterstock; 86, Joel Carillet/iStockphoto; 87, Mikael Buck; 88-89, Jody MacDonald; 90, Dorling Kindersley/Getty Images; 91, Kenneth Garrett/National Geographic Stock; 92, Sergey Gorshkov; 93 (LE UP), M. Unal Ozmen/Shutterstock; 93 (LE LO), David Quinn; 93 (RT), ostill/Shutterstock; 94-95, Michael Nichols, NGP; 96 (LE), Maggy Meyer/Shutterstock; 96 (RT), ansonsaw/iStockphoto; 97 (UP), lantapix/Shutterstock; 97 (CTR), Amelia Gaulin/National Geographic Your Shot; 97 (LO), Bettmann/Corbis; 98 (LE), Dusit/Shutterstock; 98 (RT), Gualtiero Boffi/Shutterstock; 99, Steve Path; 100-101, Zernan Labay/National Geographic Your Shot; 102, Vitaly Raduntsev/Shutterstock; 103, NASA/SDO; 104, Tim Laman/NGS; 105 (LE UP), Brian Pamphilon/iStockphoto; 105 (LE LO), David Quinn; 105 (RT—sun), designerkrim/Shutterstock; 105 (RT—Earth, Uranus, moon), Torian/Shutterstock; 106-107, John McEvoy/National Geographic Your Shot; 108 (LE), Brian J. Skerry/NGS; 108 (RT), Li Huang/Color China Photo/AP Images; 109 (UP), Roman Sotola/Shutterstock; 109 (CTR), Martin Harvey/Corbis; 109 (LO), Eric Isselee/Shutterstock; 110 (UP), Andrea Danti/Shutterstock; 110 (LO), Nicemonkey/Shutterstock; 111, PAUL MILLER/epa/Corbis; 112-113, David Stewart/National Geographic Your Shot; 114, Kenneth Garrett/NGS; 115, Vincent J. Musi/NGS; 116, Martin Schoeller/NGS; 117 (LE UP), Nikodem Nijaki/Shutterstock; 117 (LE LO), David Quinn; 117 (RT—Earth and moon), Torian/Shutterstock; 117 (RT—water), Valeriy Lebedev/Shutterstock; 118-119, Rayner Marx/National Geographic Your Shot; 120 (LE), MARIJAN MURAT/epa/Corbis; 120 (RT), Le Do/Shutterstock; 121 (UP), Lissandra Melo/Shutterstock; 121 (CTR), Jon Reed/National Geographic Your Shot; 121 (LO), Vladyslav Siaber/iStockphoto; 122 (LE), Piotr Marcinski/Shutterstock; 122 (RT), Hasloo Group Production Studio/Shutterstock; 123, Dan Callister/PacificCoastNews/Newscom; 124-125, Joel Sartore/NGS; 126, ppl/Shutterstock; 127, Joze Pojbic/iStockphoto; 128, Phyllis Galembo/NGS; 129 (LE UP), Michal Zajac/Shutterstock; 129 (LE LO), David Quinn; 129 (RT—Earth), gst/Shutterstock; 129 (RT—palace), Creative Hat/Shutterstock; 130-31, Traci Wildenstein/National Geographic Your Shot; 132 (LE), Sirsendu Gayen/National Geographic Your Shot; 132 (RT), Robert Cianflone/Getty Images; 133 (UP), NASA; 133 (LO), Cessna152/Shutterstock; 134 (UP), Moviestore Collection Ltd/Alamy; 134 (LO), Felix Mercer Moss; 135, Paul Hughes; 136-137, Rajanikanth Somasunderam/National Geographic Your Shot; 138, Eric Isselee/Shutterstock; 139, Jose Fusta Raga/Corbis; 140, Ashley Vincent; 141 (LE UP), Picsfive/Shutterstock; 141 (LE LO), David Quinn; 141 (RT—snail), Top to bottom: tomashko/Shutterstock; 141 (RT—kKoala), Eric Isselee/Shutterstock; 141 (RT—cat), Viorel Sima/Shutterstock; 141 (RT—child yawning), Antonio Guillem/Shutterstock; 141 (RT—child sleeping), Levent Konuk/Shutterstock; 142-143, Cheryl Tran/National Geographic Your Shot; 144 (LE), Andrew F. Kazmierski/Shutterstock.com; 144 (RT), Joel Sartore/NGS; 145 (UP), Klaus Kaulitzki/Shutterstock; 145 (CTR), Adriano Migliorati/Caters News Agency; 145 (CTR inset), Adriano Migliorati/Caters News Agency; 145 (LO), yui/Shutterstock; 146, Mary Evans Picture Library/Alamy; 147, Caters News/ZUMAPRESS.com/Photo via Newscom; 148-149, George Tapan/National Geographic Your Shot; 150, worker/Shutterstock; 151, Carsten Peter/Speleoresearch & Films/National Geographic Stock; 152, David Schultz/National Geographic Your Shot; 153 (LE UP), Bull's-Eye Arts/Shutterstock; 153 (LE LO), David Quinn; 153 (RT—thermometer), unkreativ/Shutterstock; 153 (RT—Uranus), Torian/Shutterstock; 153 (RT Water Molecules), 3divan/Shutterstock.

A Year With National Geographic

Yearbook 2014

Published by the National Geographic Society

John M. Fahey, *Chairman of the Board and Chief Executive Officer*

Declan Moore, *Executive Vice President; President, Publishing and Travel*

Melina Gerosa Bellows, *Executive Vice President;*
 Chief Creative Officer, Books, Kids, and Family

Prepared by the Book Division

Hector Sierra, *Senior Vice President and General Manager*

Janet Goldstein, *Senior Vice President and Editorial Director*

Jonathan Halling, *Design Director, Books and Children's Publishing*

Marianne R. Koszorus, *Design Director, Books*

R. Gary Colbert, *Production Director*

Jennifer A. Thornton, *Director of Managing Editorial*

Susan S. Blair, *Director of Photography*

Meredith C. Wilcox, *Director, Administration and Rights Clearance*

Staff for This Book

Bridget A. English, *Editor*

Anne Smyth, *Project Editor*

Melissa Farris, *Art Director*

Nancy Marion, Matt Propert, *Illustrations Editors*

Linda Makarov, *Designer*

Liz Marvin, *Picture Legends Writer*

Marshall Kiker, *Associate Managing Editor*

Judith Klein, *Production Editor*

Galen Young, *Rights Clearance Specialist*

Kristina Heitkamp, *Editorial Assistant*

Jade Polay, *Editorial Assistant*

Production Services

Phillip L. Schlosser, *Senior Vice President*

Chris Brown, *Vice President, NG Book Manufacturing*

George Bounelis, *Vice President, Production Services*

Nicole Elliott, *Manager*

Rachel Faulise, *Manager*

Robert L. Barr, *Manager*

The National Geographic Society is one of the world's largest nonprofit scientific and educational organizations. Founded in 1888 to "increase and diffuse geographic knowledge," the Society's mission is to inspire people to care about the planet. It reaches more than 400 million people worldwide each month through its official journal, *National Geographic*, and other magazines; National Geographic Channel; television documentaries; music; radio; films; books; DVDs; maps; exhibitions; live events; school publishing programs; interactive media; and merchandise. National Geographic has funded more than 10,000 scientific research, conservation and exploration projects and supports an education program promoting geographic literacy.

For more information, please call 1-800-NGS LINE (647-5463) or write to the following address:

National Geographic Society
1145 17th Street N.W.
Washington, D.C. 20036-4688 U.S.A.

For rights or permissions inquiries, please contact National Geographic Books Subsidiary Rights: ngbookrights@ngs.org

Published 2013.
Pedigree Books Limited, Beech Hill House, Walnut Gardens, Exeter, Devon EX4 4DH
www.pedigreebooks.com | books@pedigreegroup.co.uk
The Pedigree trademark, email and website addresses, are the sole and exclusive properties of Pedigree Group Limited, used under license in this publication.

13/PED/1